Case Studies in Mixed Ability Teaching

Edited by A.V. Kelly

Harper & Row, Publishers

London New York Evanston San Francisco

Copyright © 1975 Harper & Row

First published 1975
Harper & Row
28 Tavistock Street, London WC2E 7PN

Designed by 'Millions'
Typeset by Red Lion Setters, Holborn, London
Printed by Biddles of Guildford

Standard Book Number 06-318044-8 (cloth)
Standard Book Number 06-318029-4 (paper)

Contents

Introduction

Many teachers and Headteachers are currently recognising the
attraction of mixed ability groupings in Secondary schools, glimpsing
in particular their possible social and behavioural advantages, but
hesitate to take the plunge because of a fear of the practicalities of
such a change and especially a concern with its implications for the
progress of the very bright pupil. It was in an attempt to provide such
teachers with advice and assistance with some of the practical issues
that might face them that I wrote "Teaching Mixed Ability Classes".

When I wrote that book, however, although it was the result of work
done over a number of years with many teachers and student-
teachers and was thus an attempt to bring together and find generali-
sations in a wide range of experience and experimentation in mixed
ability teaching, I was conscious that a major weakness in the eyes of
many teachers would be the very fact of its attempt to generalise
rather than to give first-hand accounts of actual experiences.
Anyone who wished for any reason, therefore, to reject the ideas
expressed in that book would do so by discounting them as the
ideals of a theorist. *"Fine in theory, but impossible in practice"*
would be the response of many, some of whom would be
reluctant to embark on such changes because of genuine doubts

about the possibilities of success, others because of an unwillingness to take on voluntarily the upheavals involved in such a major change, an attitude well summed up in the advice once given to an enthusiastic student by an "experienced" woman teacher - *"Don't complicate your life, dearie!"*

A follow-up was needed to that book which would set out in detail first-hand accounts of specific schemes, written by those who in many different situations have attempted mixed ability teaching and who were prepared honestly to record their experiences, both their successes and their failures, for the benefit of others who might be about to venture into the same waters, since it is only by shared experience of this kind that real development and progress can be ensured. This book is an attempt to provide accounts of this kind. It contains reports by several Headteachers of the general issues that loom large when such a step is taken, the organisational factors and the repercussions both within and outside the school. It then goes on to offer the experience of teachers, many of them from the schools the Headteachers have described, in planning and carrying out work with such groupings in all of the major areas of the curriculum, including those in which it is often felt that mixed ability teaching is impossible, Mathematics, Science and French.

The orientation of the studies is mainly towards the Secondary school, since it is in this sector of educational provision that this issue is most controversial at present, but we have not forgotten that a Middle school philosophy is still in the early stages of its evolution, so that it cannot be assumed that an issue of this kind is as fully resolved in that sector as it seems to be in the Primary school. In fact, most of what is recorded here has relevance and application at all levels of educational provision.

Every school situation is unique and none of the contributors to this book would be happy to think that their accounts were to be taken as blueprints to be slavishly emulated by teachers in other schools. At the most they should be seen as offering evidence of what can be achieved with mixed ability groupings, guidelines as to the directions in which success may lie and perhaps also warnings as to the pitfalls that beset the path of anyone venturing into this area. We hope that others can, therefore, take heart from and adapt to their own purposes the experiences recorded here and thus achieve something of the satisfaction that every contributor acknowledges.

My own thanks are due to all who have contributed to this book. One feels that they are all people who find sufficient reward in the exercise of their professional skills. I hope it will be an added recompense for them to be aware that their experience has been made available to others on a wider scale. I hope too that they are pleased with the results of their labours and that they agree with me that our combined efforts have added up to a joint statement that not only reinforces the case for mixed ability groupings in Middle and Secondary schools but also, and more importantly, offers teachers and Headteachers a good deal of help with the practicalities of such an innovation. I am sure they will join me in hoping that this will help others to bring about such changes with a minimum of friction and that they will thus have contributed to what we believe to be a major advance in the quality of the educational experience we can offer our young people.

A.V. Kelly

London, September, 1974

The Contributors

T. Gannon, O.B.E., Headmaster of Milefield Middle School, Grimethorpe, Barnsley, South Yorkshire.

D.J. Haslam, formerly Head of Science, Sir Leo Schultz High School, Hull, Humberside.

M.R. Horne, Headmistress of Fairlop Secondary Girls' School, Hainault, Essex.

E.M. Hoyles, formerly Headmistress of Vauxhall Manor School, London, S.W.8.

A.M. Hunt, formerly Headmaster of Sir Leo Schultz High School, Hull, Humberside.

S.K. Legon, Social Studies Teacher, Fairlop Secondary Girls' School, Hainault, Essex.

B. Liddington, Head of English, Northcliffe Community High School, Conisbrough, Doncaster, Yorkshire.

P.A. Prettyman, Mathematics Teacher, Crown Woods School, London, S.E.9.

D.L. Steels, Head of Upper School Humanities, Northcliffe Community High School, Conisbrough, Doncaster, Yorkshire.

B.G. Walker, Art and Craft Advisor, Milefield Middle School, Grimethorpe, Barnsley, South Yorkshire.

R.S. Walmsley, Head of Modern Languages, Evelyns School, West Drayton, Middlesex.

A.G. Young, C.B.E., Headmaster of Northcliffe Community High School, Conisbrough, Doncaster, Yorkshire.

Mixed Ability Groups - The Key Issues

A.V. Kelly

Streaming, the practice of grouping pupils according to both chronological age and general ability, replaced the system of Standards, the
grouping of pupils by attainment only, when the establishment of
separate Primary and Secondary schools saw the gradual demise of
the all-age elementary school and the views of psychologists about
the characteristics of particular age groups made it appear undesirable
to retain classes in which the age groups could become very mixed.
At the time, it seemed to be the only effective method of ensuring
that all pupils, including both the very bright and the very backward,
received the best possible education and a "triple track system of
organisation" was given the official blessing of the Hadow Report of
1931[1] and the subsequent support of the Spens Report of 1938[2].
Its desirability was questioned, however, as early as 1945 by the
Ministry of Education[3] and the years since then have seen an
accelerating movement away from this system in both Primary and,
more recently, Secondary schools.

There are a number of reasons for this, among which can be
identified three main strands - that derived from a reassessment of
some of the theoretical considerations on which the practice was
originally based, that due to wider changes that have taken place in

our view of the aims and purposes of education, and that resulting from the evidence that has been amassed by a number of research studies. It will be worthwhile to look briefly at all these aspects of the problem if we are to be clear about the key issues that face teachers today in their search for the most satisfactory ways of grouping their pupils.

The rather naïve assumptions which underlie the system of streaming have all been brought into question by recent advances in our understanding of the processes of education and changes in our views of its nature and purposes. The assumptions behind the system seem to be that intelligence or intellectual ability is a relatively fixed and static quality which can be measured successfully; that if we group children according to their measured intelligence we will produce homogeneous teaching groups; that the main, if not the sole, concern of the school is with the development of children's cognitive abilities; that this can best be attended to by means of the class lesson, the presentation of the same material at the same level and pace to the whole class; and that this approach will be the most effective means to securing the educational progress of all pupils - the less able no less than the gifted. In connection with this last point, it is worth noting that one of the more interesting things to emerge from the research in this area has been the extent to which teachers advocate streaming on the grounds that it makes possible the establishment of small "remedial" classes, in which the less able can be given specialised attention, and ensures that such children will not be discouraged by being made to work alongside their brighter colleagues. In other words, streaming is seen as ultimately of most advantage to the less able pupil.[4]

It is the erosion of all of these fundamental assumptions that has led to a questioning of the desirability of streaming. In the first place, there are few psychologists or educationists who would wish to adhere to the simple concept of intelligence on which such reasoning is based. Intelligence is no longer regarded as the fixed or static entity that streaming implies; indeed, the current fashion is not to see it as an entity at all but as a convenient label for a continuing process of intellectual growth, and to regard it not as almost entirely determined by innate factors but as equally the product of the interaction of the individual and his environment. If we accept, then, the need for a much more fluid concept of intelligence and a full awareness of the role environmental factors can play in its development, we must question the significance of attempts to measure it and certainly the advisability of basing our groupings entirely on the results of such measurements. This has been one source, therefore, of the doubt that has come to be cast on the practice of streaming.

Secondly, the years since the 1944 Education Act have witnessed many attempts to realise the ideals encapsulated in the Act's expressed commitment to the idea of *"education for all according to age, aptitude and ability"*. A commitment to this idea implies a view of the aims and purposes of education and schooling that is very different from that which prevailed when streaming was first advocated. It implies an acceptance of the ideal expressed so well by the Crowther Report[5] that education should be the right of every child regardless of any return to society that might accrue from what has been invested in that education. This in turn suggests that a wider view must be taken of what constitutes education and of what schools should be trying to provide for their pupils and that a concern with the cognitive development of children is not enough but should be seen as only one aspect of the development that the school should attempt to promote. This again suggests that the provision of set offerings of carefully prepared subject content cannot be regarded as the only route to education in the full sense of the term. These fundamental changes in what society expects of its schools cut right across the assumptions we have suggested underlie the system of streaming and therefore make it necessary for anyone who recognises the force of them to ask whether streaming can be appropriate in such a changed situation.

It is precisely for this reason that so much attention has been directed in recent years towards making an evaluation of the effects of streaming. The results of the many studies that have contributed to this enquiry are readily available and do not need to be repeated here. Briefly, they have pointed to a number of weaknesses that can be detected in streamed systems. Many irrelevant factors, not least those associated with social class origins, enter into and render highly inaccurate the selective procedures on which it must be based; the relative effects of acceptance or rejection, praise or blame, success or failure, allied to the impact of teacher expectation and the generation of different curricula, have resulted in a minimum of transfer between streams and have therefore introduced an element of finality into the initial selection of pupils that has led to the charge that streaming is a *"self-fulfilling prophecy"*6, and that, far from catering for differences of ability, it creates such differences itself. It is thus closely linked with the problem of the relative merits of all attempts to employ selective procedures in education and especially the debate over selective systems of Secondary education. One result of this has been that streaming has been seen as a major factor in the wastage from our schools of more human talent than we can afford as a nation to lose, that was drawn to our attention by the Early Leaving Report7 and again by Crowther. In short, it has been regarded by many as a major obstacle to the achievement of anything approaching educational equality. nat. efficiency brigade.

Many studies have also highlighted its inhibiting effects on those aspects of children's development other than the academic or intellectual. There is some evidence, for example, that there is more divergent thinking in unstreamed Secondary schools.8 This evidence is not conclusive, partly because of the difficulty of measuring this kind of ability, but it is not to be ignored if we consider the development of this to be an important task for the school. Whatever the significance of this, however, there is little doubt of the effect it has on the social and emotional development of pupils. The evidence points clearly towards improved pupil-pupil and teacher-pupil relationships in unstreamed schools, along with a greater involvement of all pupils in the work and the life of the school.9 This is especially true, as one would expect, in the case of the less able and the research evidence is here confirming what every teacher has always known, namely that the rejection that is implied by allocation to a "low" stream cannot but result in disaffection, behavioural problems and ultimately on occasion even violence. Discouragement, it seems, comes not from working alongside brighter children as much as from being segregated from them. Social and emotional development are as much a function of the organisation structure of the school as of any formal provision made within it and the adverse effects of a streamed organisation on the social and emotional development of pupils are well attested at every level. Nor must we forget the effects of streaming on the morale of the teachers themselves, a point made by several of the contributors to this book.

The only factor that has encouraged the retention of streaming by many Secondary schools is the conflicting nature of the evidence of

and parents
prefer streaming
if their children
are to get on

its effects on the academic progress of pupils. In addition to being
conflicting and largely inconclusive, the evidence has also been
criticised because it is derived mainly from studies of Primary schools.
However, it is possible to suggest, if only tentatively, that certain
features do emerge from the work that has been done. The studies
suggest that unstreaming leads to no reduction in the overall levels of
attainment, that it may in fact be associated with an overall rise in
standards and that it may also result in a reduction of the spread of
attainment and ability.[10] It is the latter point that is perhaps the
most significant. A survey undertaken by the UNESCO Institute of
Education in 1962 noted the widely varying results of English school-
children when compared with those in eleven other countries and
suggested that this was due to the fact that English educationists
expect wide differences in performance. It was subsequently
suggested that this wide spread is another result of streaming[11] and
this seems to be borne out by the evidence that unstreaming may
reduce this spread. What this seems to amount to is that with non-
streaming there comes a convergence of both extremes towards the
mean; the less able do considerably better in the unstreamed school,
as one might expect if they are happier, more involved and better
motivated, but, on the other hand, the really bright pupils, the
"gifted", the "high-flyers" do less well. It is this latter feature that
has deterred many people from moving to an unstreamed form of
organisation, especially in the Secondary school.

There are two things that can be said about this. The first of these
is that we should perhaps be asking ourselves whether, even if this
picture which the evidence presents is an accurate one, we ought to
be willing to purchase the academic education of a few "gifted"
children at the cost of the social education of all pupils. This is a
question that should give us some pause and many schools which
have abandoned streaming have done so as a result of giving a very
definite answer to it. They have accepted that the social education
of their pupils is every bit as important as the academic. Whatever
position one takes on that issue, however, the second point here is a
more positive one. It is by no means certain that in the evaluation
that has been undertaken of unstreamed schools we have been
testing schools in which the methods of teaching mixed ability
classes have been fully worked out. This kind of teaching is a highly
complex matter and we should not be surprised if it takes teachers

a long time to perfect it. The evidence that the very bright have not been adequately catered for in unstreamed classes should not lead us to believe that their needs cannot be attended to, not at least until considerably more attention has been given to the development of appropriate methods for teaching such classes. Several of the contributors to this book admit that they have not yet solved the problem of the very bright pupil but they all feel that a solution can be found.

The focus of attention in the streaming debate has now shifted, therefore, from questions of its merits and defects to questions about how innovations like unstreaming come about in schools and about how teachers can set about the task of developing appropriate methods to cater adequately for the education of all pupils in the mixed ability class. Some light is thrown incidentally on the first of these issues in this book, but it is on the latter question that we concentrate in an attempt to contribute to the generation of a methodology of mixed ability teaching.

If unstreaming is to have a chance of succeeding so that we can get off the horns of the dilemma presented to us by the twin concerns for the social and academic aspects of education, then we must get our methods right and there are several factors that must be taken full account of as we set about this task. These factors emerge very clearly in the case studies that follow but it is worth drawing them together here. As we do so, one preliminary point must be stressed. The studies reveal a number of different approaches that have been adopted; there is more than one way to skin any cat and it is clear that there are many different forms that a mixed ability organisation can take and that it must be adapted to the local conditions that apply in each particular situation. It is vital, therefore, that these studies should not be regarded as blueprints from which schools or individual teachers can select the model they will follow. Each school and each teacher must work out his own solution to his own unique situation. This, after all, is what professionalism implies. Certain general points do emerge from the studies, however, which all such teachers and Headteachers may find useful as guidelines.

In the first place, it is apparent that little of value will come from the introduction of mixed ability groupings if attention is not given to the establishment of an organisational structure that will support such a development. This will involve replanning at a number of levels. A traditional kind of Secondary school time-table will not support and may even hinder the teacher in his efforts to adjust to the demands of the new situation. Flexibility becomes very important so that time-tabling for flexibility is vital. Opportunities must be built into the structure for varying the groupings, the activities and the content of the work. In practice this will mean a blocking of the time-table - often actually easier to do than to cater for seven or eight different periods every day - and allocation of adequate and varied accommodation for use during these blocked times by the mixed ability groups. It will also mean that a lot of attention must be given to the availability of specialist accommodation such as library and workshop facilities and to the provision of a wide range of resources. In many cases it has also proved desirable to reorganise the basic structure and even the hierarchy of the school by introducing new groupings such as tutor-groups and new posts of responsibility such as year tutors, team or project leaders and advisory specialists. In many ways these are the inevitable results of a concern with the social and pastoral dimensions of schooling. Their introduction in conjunction with a move to mixed ability teaching merely serves to underline this aspect of that development. Some reorganisation must be undertaken, however, to provide an institutional framework which will be more suited to this new approach and will help teachers to take full advantage of it.

A second factor that has clearly been of great significance to some Headteachers as they have made changes of this kind has been the attitude of parents to what was going on. Indeed, Margaret Horne goes so far as to speak of the "wrath" of a few of her parents, and such a reaction is not lessened in importance or impact by the awareness that those parents who displayed feelings of this kind were those *"whose children would have been 'A' but who were now unlabelled"*. It is very natural for parents to be concerned at the possible repercussions of this kind of drastic change of approach on the education of their children, especially in the light of the uninformed alarmism of the press and the media in relation to educational "progressivism", and this concern must be allayed if the confidence and support of parents is to be obtained. Such confidence and support can best be won by putting parents fully into the picture, by telling them clearly what one is hoping to achieve and perhaps even by involving them severally or collectively in some of the work itself. For there are positive opportunities here, since this can be the beginning of the kind of involvement of outsiders of many kinds in the life and work of the school that Tom Gannon, for example, advocates when he tells us of the advantages of regarding the term "parent" as including *"all other responsible relatives of the children and indeed any persons disposed to show interest in the school's welfare".* If the idea of the community school has any merit, it must surely start here, and the range of outsiders willing to become involved in the work of the school is clear from Don Steels' account of the "Third Seminar" at Northcliffe Community High School.

Of equal importance, of course, are the attitudes of individual members of staff. We must never forget how crucial the support of the teacher is to the success of any scheme; unstreaming can only work when the teachers believe in it[12]. A number of consequences would seem to follow from this. To begin with, it would suggest the advisability of limiting the introduction of mixed ability classes to those areas or subjects for which there exists in the school an adequate number of enthusiastic or willing teachers and of being aware, as Andrew Hunt tells us, that we should never *"foist mixed ability teaching willy-nilly on uncertain and unready colleagues".* In many cases, of course, such an innovation will in fact be a direct result of pressures brought to bear on the Head by a group of enthusiastic teachers and clearly they are the ones to be given the first chance to try out their schemes. There is another side to this, however, that one has seen too often and that no Headteacher can afford to ignore. *"Uncertain and unready colleagues",* whether involved in the work or not, can quickly become what Margaret Horne calls *"sceptical saboteurs"* and if we give some enthusiastic teachers their heads or even ask them to try out something new for us, we owe it to them to protect them as far as possible from such attempts to make their task even more difficult than it already is.

With this in mind, we should note the step-by-step possibilities that a move to mixed ability groupings offers, so as to ensure, in Arthur Young's phrase, that it is *"evolutionary not revolutionary".* The advisability of a gradual development is clear and the kind of flexible time-table we have already referred to should make possible its initial introduction in a modified form through a "broad banding" system and/or in certain years only and/or in certain subjects only. In nearly all schools, as the case studies will show, there have been certain subjects for which Headteachers have had to maintain some kind of grouping by ability, usually by some form of setting, and it is equally clear that this is not due to anything endemic in those subjects themselves, since there is no uniformity of practice; it is entirely a matter of personality factors and of the attitudes of individual teachers. These must be respected, so that a phased introduction of mixed ability groupings, which may in any case be desirable, becomes doubly so in the light of this kind of consideration.

Those teachers who are involved in the first stages of such schemes need a great deal of support. Much of the success of the schemes described in this book derives from the fact that teachers were involved in the planning of them from the outset, so that they were in every sense their own schemes. This is the only way to ensure continued "on the spot" planning. They need the confidence and freedom to experiment, to adapt and to learn the lessons of the new way of working and this can only be theirs if they do not have to go in fear of the consequences of any mistakes they may make and if they enjoy from the beginning the full support and backing of the Headteacher. They need his protection not only against sceptical colleagues but also in situations where their work must be explained to parents or to governors or to local authority officials. This in turn requires a new and different pattern of relationships within the school. Where schemes of this kind have been successful, it is plain that relationships between teacher and teacher and, in particular, those between teacher and Head are founded on mutual trust and respect rather than on any hierarchical structure or clear division of responsibility. All are working together towards common goals and each accepts the role of the other as complementary.

This is one aspect of a total change in the pattern of relationships that will occur in the school as a whole, since the move to mixed ability groupings will be motivated, as we have seen, at least in part by a change in our view of the aims and purposes of education and a greater concern with the pastoral and social dimensions of schooling. However, if these social advantages are not to be purchased at the price of the academic attainment of any pupils, whether "gifted" or any other, steps must be taken to ensure that staff have the opportunity and the encouragement to acquire the new skills and competences that will be required of them. The advantages that have accrued from the provision by some local authorities of in-service courses to support this kind of development in schools are apparent and there is no doubt that where such backing has been provided the transition to mixed ability groupings has been eased considerably. There cannot be enough of this kind of provision. A lot can also be done and has been done by Colleges of Education in preparing trainee teachers for this kind of work, but there is no doubt that the focus of professional training must be the classroom itself and, since there are still not enough schools working in this way to enable colleges to give every student this kind of experience, it is unavoidable that for some time to come many teachers will continue to leave the Colleges and Departments of Education unprepared for and without experience of this kind of teaching. Whatever the in-service provision, therefore, it is important, as Elizabeth Hoyles tells us, for each school within itself *"to mount a considerable in-service training programme"*. We must be fully aware of the need both to train experienced teachers to meet the different demands of the new situation and to continue to train new entrants to the profession in the skills that will now be demanded of them, although it is worth noting the incidental training that goes on when teachers are working closely with each other.

The precise nature of these new skills and competences also emerges clearly from the case studies that follow. It becomes apparent that, regardless of the particular subject areas they are concerned with, certain common problems have faced all teachers, even though their solutions to them have varied to suit their own individual requirements. It will be helpful to identify these general problems to enable teachers to focus their attention on what seem to be the main points of impact of the change to mixed ability groupings.

The first and most fundamental requirement of all teachers in catering for mixed ability classes is a deep understanding of the educative process. More responsibility for educational decision making devolves on the individual teacher in this kind of situation then in one where he is working to a set syllabus, with perhaps set books and set methods, the responsibility for which rests elsewhere. It is apparent from all of these studies that a great deal of rethinking of a very basic kind has been demanded of every teacher. As we have seen, the trend to mixed ability groupings is itself a product of

fundamental re-thinking about the purposes of education, in
particular a re-examination of some well established presuppositions,
such as those about the nature of intelligence and educational ability.
We must also remember that this trend is one feature of a more
general process of curriculum development. In practice it will be
found to be inextricably linked with other kinds of curriculum
change, such as the introduction of new "subjects" into the
curriculum, like the entomology, judo and calligraphy that Tom
Gannon mentions, or perhaps a move towards some form of integrated
studies. It will, therefore, necessitate a rethinking of all aspects of
the curriculum, objectives and content as well as methods or
procedures, both at a general level and in relation to specific subjects.

Every contributor to this book has indicated the extent to which a
complete re-evaluation of his or her work has become necessary. Two
things follow from this. In the first place, we can perhaps begin to
see more clearly than hitherto how the theoretical study of education
should be related to its practice. For such rethinking, if it is to have
any value or lead to any satisfactory changes, must be theoretically
sound as well as practically viable. In this connection it is worth
mentioning the advantages that one or two contributors refer to of
links they have been able to forge with local Colleges of Education.
The way to improved training procedures and professional advance-
ment for all teachers lies here, I am sure. Secondly, it highlights the
need for all teachers to be willing and able to alter their methods and
approach quite radically. Again the changes that this will lead to
must be tailored to the individual situation and some of them will
be specific to certain subject areas and can be left to the studies
themselves. It is the general directions of these changes that I must
draw attention to.

Whether it is accepted that the content of the work to be done
should be decided in the light of what appear to be the needs and
the interests of individual pupils or whether some kind of common
syllabus is retained, it is plain that the move to mixed ability
groupings must be accompanied by an individualising of method, of
the level of work and of the pace at which the ground is covered.
In other words, although, as several contributors stress, the class
lesson still has its part to play, it will often give way to more informal
ways of working in which individual pupils or groups of pupils will
be working at their own particular tasks. All of the demands that

mixed ability groupings make of the teacher are consequent on this basic feature of the approach needed by such groups.

The immediate impact of the individual approach is felt in the need for the provision of varied resources. All teachers are aware of how important it is to have material ready so that each class can be settled down to work quickly and with a minimum of fuss; the problem of doing this is much greater when they are not all settling down to the same activity. Furthermore, almost every contributor to this book has drawn our attention to the paucity of material that is available at present for use with mixed ability groups. In some ways this is not such a bad thing since, whatever the publishers offer or come to offer to the teacher, adaptation to the needs of his own pupils remains the teacher's responsibility, but at the moment the problem is greater in so far as there is little that is ready to hand even for such adaptation. In some areas there is useful material available such as the packs provided by the Humanities Curriculum Project, which, as Don Steels shows, can be adapted to particular situations, and the Scottish Integrated Science worksheets and Nuffield Secondary Science material which David Haslam was able to modify and combine with his own, but good quality material like this is not readily to hand in all areas.

The solution that most teachers have found here, therefore, has been the preparation of their own material and in particular, work-cards of various kinds and at various levels of difficulty. A great deal of ingenuity has been shown in the composition of these word-cards and teachers may find the example given by Phil Prettyman and David Haslam helpful guides when they set about preparing their own. The production of an adequate range of work-cards is only a beginning, however. There must also be books and resource materials of all kinds, including in some cases equipment for practical work, and the studies also contain some useful tips on how these can be provided and a supply of such material built up. There is no doubt that a resources centre is vital and the linking of this with the school library will prove a further advantage, especially if pupils can be given training in the use of this kind of facility through the library lesson or increased access to it through a decentralisation of the library of the kind that Bruce Liddington describes. The development of a bank of resources of this kind will be a continuing process. Once such a bank is established, provided that access to what it contains can be made easy, it should be possible to keep children busily occupied even if the work of any class is very varied. In the initial stages of the change to mixed ability groupings, however, the preparation of suitably varied resources materials is a major task for every teacher, although it can be eased if they are prepared by a team of teachers. We must also in this connection remember Elizabeth Hoyles' warning that shoddily produced resources will encourage a low standard of work from the children.

We must not forget too that pupils may need to be trained in this way of working by themselves or in groups, although it may be that many of them will have become familiar with it in their Primary schools. This will need to have some of our attention and we should perhaps see it as part of the wider problem of keeping an eye on and up to date records of the work and progress of each individual child. We need to know what each individual has done and what ground he has covered. We need to know this both in order to be able to decide what he should do next and in order to ensure that he is in fact working in a purposeful way. Although it is clear that mixed ability groupings lead to improved behaviour and attitudes to work, it would be a mistake to assume that they lead to the total disappearance of the lazy pupil. We have all heard stories of the child who does the same project every week or every term and thus avoids breaking any new ground, and Shirley Legon reminds us that there are pupils who will go out of the school ostensibly to carry out research but in fact to loaf about the neighbourhood. This problem is even more serious within team-teaching programmes, where one teacher can be "played off" against another, and one important function of regular and formal meetings of the staff involved in these programmes is to close all such loopholes. This kind of danger can only be obviated by the keeping of full and adequate records of each child's work. This also makes possible continuous check on each individual's progress and this has more positive advantages if confirmation of achievement can be provided for the child himself, since this should enhance motivation and encourage further effort.

A further major consideration for teachers of mixed ability groups is the change in relationships that this looser kind of class organisation engenders. There is general agreement among teachers that discipline problems are reduced, if only by a distribution of those children whose levels of achievement and of motivation are low throughout all classes rather than a concentration of them in one or two groups, and that there is an improvement in the attitudes of pupils towards the school, a claim which, as we saw earlier, supports some of the research evidence in this area.[9] There is also general agreement that the new kinds of relationship between teachers and pupils which can evolve are more satisfying to teachers and ultimately, one would therefore think, better for the pupils than those normally associated with streamed classes.

As many of the studies show, the pupils recognise, especially when the changes are explained to them, that they are in a school that cares about every one of them and it is this single factor that is at the root of the improved attitudes that everyone comments on. Equally, however, it must be stressed that the development of relationships of this kind places added strain on the expertise of the teacher. They will not evolve satisfactorily without a great deal of help from him, and they will depend to a large extent on his own attitudes to his work and his pupils and on the degree of expertise he shows both in relation to his knowledge of his subject and his skill in handling children. In other words, his authority must have a different basis; it must be founded on expertise rather than on position; and this is something else that all teachers must be aware of and must be ready to work at if they are to make a success of mixed ability teaching.

This is another aspect of that changing pattern of relationships in the school as a whole that we have already referred to, a change to what David Haslam calls an *"open doors"* philosophy. Whether the move to mixed ability groupings is accompanied by the development of team-teaching or not - and the studies make it clear how often such a development does follow, either within a subject or between subjects - it leads inevitably to more interaction between teachers and to greater collaboration at a number of different levels. The studies reveal how much more teachers are engaged in working with each other, some show the advantage of involving parents and others from outside the school in the children's work and in general the picture is one in which the individual teacher's total autonomy within the four walls of his own classroom is considerably eroded and his role becomes a more flexible one. There are many grounds on which such a development can be welcomed, some of which the studies highlight. What must be stressed here, however, is that it is another source of pressure on the teacher, another area in which he must rethink his position and adapt to changed circumstances.

There is no doubt, however, that what worries teachers most as they contemplate this kind of change and, indeed, what often deters them from undertaking it, is a concern for the welfare of exceptional pupils, both the "gifted" and the "backward". Many teachers feel that it will be possible to cater for neither adequately in a mixed ability class. The evidence, as we have seen, gives some support to this view in relation to "gifted" pupils but none at all in relation to the backward, who clearly seem to do better by any criteria in mixed ability classes. An acceptance of the need to make individual provision is a step towards meeting the needs of pupils at both extremes of the ability range, provided that we are aware of the importance of catering adequately for all pupils. This implies that we must prepare work-cards and resources of all kinds at a number of different levels of difficulty and complexity. This emerges very clearly in many of these studies and it is particularly worth noting in this connection the idea, discussed very fully by Phil Prettyman in relation to the teaching of Mathematics, of providing work-cards that involve repetition for those who need it and others that extend the work to an advanced level for those capable and in need of being further stretched. We must also remember that there is a great deal that is valuable that even the non-reader can do and we must be prepared to provide opportunities for work other than of a written kind for these pupils.

It is clear, however, that most people have found that specific needs, and especially those for such things as special help with reading difficulties, cannot be adequately catered for within the normal class situation. Nor perhaps should we be attempting too seriously to deal with such problems here, since we run the risk of allowing this kind of weakness to colour and spoil all of the experiences the child has at school. The system that is generally favoured is one of withdrawal of pupils for special help of this kind, sometimes to outside centres. Nor is there any reason why the withdrawal of the "backward" for this kind of help should not be paralleled by a withdrawal of the "gifted" for advanced provision in those particular areas where their giftedness manifests itself.[12] The great advantage of a mixed ability organisation is that it provides a secure flexible basis for further groupings of all kinds. It is a far more subtle tool, if used properly, than the rather blunt instrument of streaming.

This whole question of the wide range of ability that will be included in any one mixed ability class comes to a head, of course, as we get nearer to the time at which the pupils must submit themselves to various kinds of external assessment. This is another major concern of teachers as they contemplate a move towards mixed ability groupings and again one that has deterred many from such a move. We must turn finally, therefore to a consideration of some of the solutions that teachers have found for this problem.

Before we do so, it may be worth noting a general feature of assessment that several contributors stress, namely the need to view it from the point of view of the effort and progress of the individual in relation to his own previous achievements rather than by comparison with the achievement of others, and to express it in comments rather than in literal or numerical marks or grades. In other words, it is being suggested that the ethos of mixed ability grouping is one that demands a cooperative rather than a competitive approach to education. This requires of us new attitudes towards assessment, a rethinking at both the theoretical and the practical levels of its nature and purposes and an awareness of the need to measure children against themselves rather than against each other. The measure of the individual's progress is the improvement in the standard of his own work rather than a comparison between his work and that of his colleagues. Thus assessment is seen as having a positive and encouraging role to play in the education of all pupils rather than proving a discouragement to many. Such an approach will also lead to our taking account of a wider range of achievements and qualities than purely academic attainment, it will encourage the inclusion of many other elements on the curriculum, such as those that Brian Walker describes in the field of Art and Craft, and it may result in our being able to provide anyone who needs it with much more relevant and useful information about the strengths and qualities of each child. In this kind of process, it may also be worthwhile to explore the possibilities of self-assessment, as Phil Prettyman suggests, and of helping children to acquire the power of judgement necessary to assess their own performances on which Elizabeth Hoyles sets such store. Here, as elsewhere, there are large and possibly fruitful areas for exploration.

An approach of this kind may be totally appropriate for internal assessment within the school and may ensure that such procedures have more meaning and purpose than many of the rituals that some Secondary schools celebrate once or twice a year. It cannot, however, be entirely appropriate to the external examination, whose whole *raison d'être* is the application of national standards to each pupil's attainment and thus inevitably the comparison of each individual with his fellows. It is this that has caused teachers most trouble and this that, more than any other single factor, has delayed the introduction of mixed ability groupings in many Secondary schools, in the same way as the 11+ delayed the same development in Junior schools. Indeed, many Secondary schools that have introduced mixed ability groupings in the first years have found it impossible to maintain these beyond the third year because of the pressures of external examinations. On the other hand, many have been equally reluctant to abandon methods that seem to have made good sense in the early years, to lose the advantages that they feel have accrued from these mixed ability groupings and in particular to reintroduce the behavioural problem of the "C" and "D" classes, particularly when, with the raising of the school leaving age to sixteen, the rejection that streaming implies is likely to be most damaging to the individual, the class and the school itself.

This problem of external examinations is, then, perhaps the most crucial to the development of mixed ability teaching and we must give it careful attention. In particular it is here that we have most to learn from the case studies and their accounts of the solutions some teachers have found to this difficulty. Broadly speaking, there are two kinds of solution, those that involve the introduction at this stage of some kind of grouping by ability other than streaming and those that have attempted to adapt the examination procedures themselves to the new purposes that the mixed ability groupings create.

A grouping by ability that should not be accompanied by the social disadvantages we have already referred to can be achieved in the upper reaches of the Secondary school in a number of ways. To begin with, pupils have a realistic view of their own capabilities by this stage and this is likely to be especially true if they have had the advantages of helpful and enlightened internal assessment procedures and if they have not suffered the total discouragement of early rejection on the grounds of inferior ability. In most Secondary schools they can be trusted, therefore, with proper tutorial guidance to make sensible choices among the options available to them, so that a kind of natural grouping based on self-selection can be envisaged at this stage. Furthermore, where these guided choices result in large groups so that some sub-division becomes necessary, a division based on attainment in that specific subject or field becomes possible and this is regarded by many people as being an acceptable solution to this problem. There is a real difference which we must not forget between *streaming* on the basis of some vague notion of general ability, which results in the production of one grouping for all purposes, and *setting* according to attainment in a particular subject and only for lessons in that subject. Divisions of this kind, sometimes into groups aiming at either GCE or CSE awards, have been adopted by many schools as a solution to this problem. As we have remarked already, the mixed ability group can and should be a basis for many different subsidiary groupings.

Where this kind of solution has been adopted, several other factors have emerged that are of considerable importance to our general theme and these come out particularly clearly in Richard Walmsley's account of his arrangements for teaching French in the upper school. In the first place, as he makes clear, there are advantages in grouping pupils according to interest as well as attainment, in gathering together not only those most able in the subject but also those most highly motivated towards the study of it. Indeed, several contributors comment on the advantages of grouping pupils according to interest, industry and even personality. Secondly, he also stresses that the composition of these "top" sets is different when they are built onto a mixed ability organisation in the lower school since many able and interested pupils are "scooped up" by the mixed ability classes who in a streamed system might have languished in the lower streams, suffering from all the disadvantages of a low teacher expectation, and might never have discovered either their interest in or talent for a subject such as French. A similar experience is recorded by Arthur Young in relation to those pupils who achieved success in the combined GCE and CSE Humanities course at Northcliffe Community High School. Thirdly, setting of this kind enables us to offer different kinds of examination programme even within the same subject, not only separate GCE and CSE courses, but also, for example, French language and European Studies courses. Since the pressures of external examinations must limit the extent to which our provision can be individualised at this level, opportunities for providing variety of this kind must not be rejected too lightly.

The second solution that some have found to the problem of the impact of external examination procedures has been, as we suggested, to modify and adapt these procedures to their own purposes. From the beginning, Mode 3 of the CSE has made possible a certain amount of continued individualisation of programmes and both Mode 2 and Mode 3 have given the teachers themselves the kind of share in and influence on the examination procedures that they must have if they are to have the confidence to experiment and try new approaches. They have also provided that variety of examining techniques that is equally crucial. These are the major features of the modifications necessary if the public examination system is not to necessitate a reintroduction of grouping by ability in the last years of schooling, and, as the studies show, full use has been made of the opportunities that the CSE regulations provide for all of these by those concerned to maintain a mixed ability form of organisation throughout the Secondary school. Such opportunities do not exist to the same extent within the GCE, however, and the mere fact that GCE and CSE Boards are separate bodies makes added difficulties for schools and seems to render some division of pupils almost essential. Some schools have attempted to solve this by entering all pupils for both examinations or by delaying selection of them until the examination entries themselves have to be made half-way through the final year, but by far the most interesting and hopeful development is the production of combined GCE and CSE syllabuses and examinations of the kind being pioneered at Northcliffe Community High School. Schemes of this kind may help to pave the way for the introduction of a common system of examining at 16+ along the lines suggested by the Schools Council.[13] It is in this direction that a solution must be sought for the problem of getting the right kind of assessment procedures for a mixed ability organisation. Decisions about examination procedures logically should follow rather than precede decisions about curriculum content and the methods we feel it appropriate to adopt. As Margaret Horne says, *"the examinations used must reflect the education provided.".*

These are the foremost current concerns of those who have adopted a mixed ability form of organisation. The studies in this book may indicate to teachers some of the ways in which they might set about dealing with them in the context of their own school, subject or classroom. They also show that this form of organisation has a great deal to contribute in all situations, even in those subjects for which many teachers feel a fairly rigid form of streaming is essential. What is vital is that we recognise the need for flexibility of groupings and do not adhere slavishly to any one pattern whatever it is based on. It is clear too from the studies that in the last analysis it is the attitudes of individual teachers and Headteachers that is crucial.

However, if there is one basic lesson to be learned from these accounts it is the need for continued thinking and development. None of the contributors feels that a final solution has been reached. As Shirley Legon tells us, *"It is necessary and vital to go on working at better ways of organising courses to meet the needs of the whole ability range"*. Indeed, all are conscious of the dangers of regarding any scheme as a new orthodoxy, as a static solution rather than as the kind of dynamic ongoing development that seems more appropriate to education in a changing world.

If there is to be continued development, it is clear that a lot of work still remains to be done at the level of general theory and in the context of individual schools. A lot must be done by teachers in preparation for a major change of this kind. Only when much more spadework of the kind described in these pages has been done, will it be possible to make a proper and fair evaluation of mixed ability teaching, since only then will it have begun to reach a full stature. One thing is clear, however, even at this stage and that is the enhanced professional satisfaction of those who have made real efforts to make this system work. Whatever reservations they have about the current state of this development and the teething troubles they have themselves experienced with it, none of them would return to a streamed form of organisation.

But it is time to let them speak for themselves.

References

1 Primary Education (HMSO 1931)

2 Spens Report (HMSO 1938)

3 The Nations's Schools (Ministry of Education Pamphlet No. 1., 1945)

4 cf. Daniels J.C., The Effects of Streaming in the Primary School - What Teachers Believe, British Journal of Educational Psychology, 1961.

5 15 to 18 (HMSO 1959)

6 cf. Jackson, B., Streaming: an education system in miniature (RKP 1964)

7 Early Leaving (HMSO 1954)

8 See Ferri, E., Streaming: Two Years Later (NFER 1972)

9 See Barker-Lunn, J.C., Streaming in the Primary School (NFER 1970)

10 See Daniels, J.C., The Effects Of Streaming in the Primary School - A Comparison of Streamed and Unstreamed Schools, British Journal of Educational Psychology, 1961

11 See Jackson, B. op. cit. pp. 122 ff.

12 cf. James, C.M. Young Lives at Stake (Collins 1968) Ch. 6.

13 Schools Council Examinations Bulletin No. 23., A Common System of Examining at 16+ (Evans/Methuen Educational 1971)

Part I
The Heads and the Schools

Chapter 1
Northcliffe Community High School

A.G. Young, C.B.E.

To explain changes we have made in the curriculum of this school
over the last decade, it will be necessary for me to tell you something
of its background, the philosophy of its teachers and our plans for
the future. Northcliffe is a community High school with just over
1,100 good natured rumbustious Yorkshire kids on roll between the
ages of elevent and sixteen - most of them the sons and daughters of
the miners who dig our coal for us from the South Yorkshire pits.
The school serves the old historic town of Conisbrough, landmarked
by its ruined Norman Castle, and the colliery district of Denaby Main,
landmarked by its enormous slag heap. Together these form an urban
area with a population of 17,000, clearly separated from the
neighbouring towns of Mexborough and Doncaster by the windings
of the River Don and stretches of farmland. Northcliffe is the only
Secondary school serving the township, so that whatever community
links we forge can be very properly related to the total needs of the
locality, more or less uncomplicated by considerations of what
other Secondary schools may be offering in other parts of the
Authority. The school has a unique integration scheme with a
boarding school in Devon - Dartington Hall School, famed for its
liberal progressive-school methods - and shares a residential annexe

called "The Terrace" set up by Dartington at Conisbrough. There is a regular exchange of scholars between the two schools throughout the year. One obvious feature of the school is the very strong outward bound tradition based on the Duke of Edinburgh Awards. There is a transport section of three vehicles - two Safari Landrovers and a Bedford Minibus, - to cater for Duke of Edinburgh expeditions and other school journeyings, and we have contrived so far to run these classrooms on wheels entirely out of school funds.

We are housed in overcrowded buildings put up in 1929. The classrooms are arranged round three grassed courtyards. One of the courts houses a small zoo, another the school's canoes and sailing dinghies, the third is a play area. Major extensions to provide much needed community facilities are beng built - there will be a large sports complex, open plan areas for integrated studies and team teaching, with resource facilities, project areas for the practical subjects, and a restaurant and shop attached to the housecraft rooms. The scale of social provision will be unusual with a coffee bar and lounge for each of the year groups - five altogether - and this should have a very civilizing effect on behaviour generally. We have gone a long way in this direction already, and long breaks in morning and afternoon sessions with thoughtful provisions for games and music are much appreciated by all concerned. Just as much work and study gets done in the long run, I am sure.

Two fields in which the school has pioneered over the past years should be mentioned if you are to understand the background to the unstreaming and curriculum reform with which this study is concerned. One is the extension of the school day by a voluntary third session from 6.30pm to 9.00pm on four nights a week, Mondays to Thursdays, and the other is a very considerable involvement in conservation schemes for improving the environment. The extended day provides the boys and girls with educational and recreational opportunities they would otherwise miss, and about a third of them avail themselves of these facilities. It must be significant that I have observed boys who have truanted from school during the day turning up for the voluntary third session — proving quite a number of things. Our involvement with environmental conservation, for which there is such need in this despoiled part of the country, has taken the school into both the finals of the national competitions so far sponsored by Nature Conservancy and Shell. In Conservation Year 1970, the team from Northcliffe were runners up in the competition and Shell sent them on a week's tour of the Continental conservation sites as a reward for their efforts. In 1972 our team won first place in the finals and brought back a £500 prize which paid for one of our Landrovers.

I will try to complete the setting for you by telling you of the most exciting development we are engaged upon - an experiment in quite unorthodox alternative education for some of the sixteen year olds of the RSLA group who are unable or unwilling to follow examination courses. This alternative route takes the boys and girls out of school practically all the time. They form a "club" at the Terrace, organize their programme with only a little help from adults and involve themselves in "earning and learning" situations making money from various commissions and community projects which give them a real sense of fulfilment. The fact that none of them has dropped out of the scheme or played truant speaks for itself. De-schooling? Much would depend on what your definition of education might be. To the traditionalist I suppose it would look very much like it - but why should we leave radical solutions for desperate situations to the de-schoolers when the English system of education gives us so much freedom to manoeuvre?

From the foregoing you will have begun to realise that social education has a very high priority at Northcliffe - certainly ranking as highly as academic education in all our planning. Many of us believe that the future needs of the people and the country can only be met in this way. Relationships within the cosmos of the school are all important - they are based on democratic procedures and controls rather than on any system of sanctions or punishments. The informality and natural rapport which arises from an absence of punishment and prefectorial systems is rewarding and rarely abused. The freedom of our boys and girls to dress as they choose and style their hair as they think best is all part of the same philosophy of education and, as this is a case study, must be taken into account. Hardly a traditional establishment, is it? But we would claim that it suits the needs of the locality it serves better this way. We would not claim this to be the only way nor would we expect general agreement with our methods, but in spite of all the apparent relaxation and freedom we give the boys and girls, our end results in public examinations are as good as they ever were before, and the incidence of aggressive behaviour has been greatly reduced.

In tracing the pattern of reforms which we have carried out over the past fifteen years it should be very significant that the first of these was a move towards unstreaming and mixed ability grouping - the broad banding of year groups into two bands of ability. Scrambling the "A's" and "B's" together and the "C's" and "D's", while maintaining a small remedial class. We might have gone all the way to complete unstreaming, but there was a cautious feeling among the staff, who still saw children in the first forms as potential or non-potential GCE candidates five years on, and they needed to get used to the idea that it was not really a game of chess that depended on the right opening gambit. But then the process of change at this school has all been gradual and pragmatical, evolutionary rather than revolutionary. Perhaps that is why we have got so far along the line without opposition from the authorities or staff reaction. Perhaps it would become clearer if I gave you a list of these inter-related changes in some sort of chronological order:

1959 (Boys' School then separate from Girls' School) Introduction of Duke of Edinburgh Awards. Establishment of outward bound tradition and purchase of two 5 ton ex-WD Bedford infantry trucks. School traditionally streamed A B C D.

1962 *Introduction of broad banding.* Two forms in "top" band, two in lower band with small remedial form. A B C D nomenclature abandoned in favour of house names. Nobody fooled by this but some of the stigmatizations disappearing.

1963 Introduction of Voluntary Homework in School. Embryonic third session. First group of boys through GCE "O" level exams.

1964 (a) Amalgamation of separate schools to form one mixed Secondary Modern with 975 pupils on roll. Boys and girls brought together in all classes except fifth year GCE which for this year was boys only. Broad banding now in second, third and fourth years.
(b) *Unstreamed mixed ability groups established in all eight first year forms* with arrangements for help to be given to backward readers on an extraction basis.

1966 Humanities Projects integrating English, Geography, History and Religious Education introduced to the non-examination forms in the fourth year with block timetabling and team-teaching.

1967 Humanities Projects, team-teaching and block timetabling established for the eight first year forms and the eight second year forms with plans to "grow" the system throughout the school. School Committee formed with boy and girl representation from each form - able to debate any matter.

1969 Formation of exchange link with Dartington Hall School. Purchase of "The Terrace" as a joint residential annexe. Conservation schemes started.

1970 Acceptance by both CSE and GCE Boards of a common syllabus in the Humanities for Mode 3 continuous assessment and certification in four subject areas. Second place in finals of Nature Conservancy Competition.

1972 First place in national finals of Nature Conservancy Competition.

1973 First group of scholars through new Humanities examination. General agreement that many would never have entered for examination under traditional system of streaming by ability.

1974 The year of the raising of the school leaving age. Still holding to unstreaming throughout the school but with many options available to fourth and fifth formers, and a completely Alternative School course for a voluntary group outside school at the Terrace - earning and learning. Block timetabling, team-teaching and mixed ability forms throughout the school.

I think you will be able to see what a vital part unstreaming has played in the social and educational development of the school and I imagine that you may have noted the growth points in its implementation which have occurred at definite stages in the school's history. Such a bald statement of development ignores the extensive programme of in service training and staff conferences, parent-teachers' meetings and Examination Board committees which have taken place along the way. Nor does it make clear to you why the changes we have made seemed desirable. What were the observable

effects of the changes on the boys and girls at the receiving end? For
some of the answers we shall have to go back quite a few years to
look for the reasons which impelled us towards working with mixed
ability groups.

Why Unstreaming?

There was a general feeling of dissatisfaction among the staff at the
social consequences produced by our "sheep and goats" act. Many
felt that we were guilty of extending the evil social division caused
by the 11+ examination by our further invidious separations. We had
had consciences about social apartheid systems in education. Elitist
systems jangled badly with our sense of democratic fair play, made
keener by our recent struggle with the Nazis. Our arbitrary divisions
amongst the children turned out to be self-fulfilling prophecies - for
rarely were kids moved from one stream to another because we
admitted our prognosis to be wrong. Those of us who were honest
doubted whether this absence of movement really proved that we
were so God-almighty right and infallible at this "ABCD" business.
We suspected rather that the brightest and most alert were flattered
and spurred on to greater effort by the comforting knowledge that
they were the Chosen Ones - the ones who would be successful all
through life. Nothing less was implied by being in the "A" stream.
The "B" streamers plodded on without much enthusiasm but
without much resistance either - this was expected of them. The "C"
and "D" streamers knew they were regarded as the "thickies" and,
expected to behave badly, they played their roles with reactive
stupidity, fooling themselves as well as their teachers. We knew this
was a false situation. How was it that many of these same dull and
backward ones would confound all prophecy shortly after leaving
school by passing their driving tests first time, while many of the
chosen ones would need three or four tries before they were through?
And to see some of them doing quick arithmetic behind the market
stalls was disconcerting to say the least. Of course there was always
the "late developer" excuse to fall back on if we were unscrupulous.

There were other aspects of "ABCD" which led to inevitable
difficulties. The matching disciplinary patterns were also self-
fulfilling prophecies. "A" to "D" in ability synchronised almost
exactly with "A" to "D" in behaviour. Like most Headmasters, I also
found it necessary to match staff to these requirements. The most

imaginative and sensitive teachers for the "A's", almost anyone would be able to manage the "B's", the toughest and most insensitive for the "C's" and thank God for volunteers - very often indeed the most dedicated ones - for the "D's". We also had the evidence of the Duke of Edinburgh Awards which puzzled us greatly, for here was a scheme organised in such a way that it should appeal to young people of all abilities - yet it was not found to work in this way for us. We were finding that although we started with groups from all streams, most of the "C" and "D" streamers were dropping out after only a few weeks. Another case of the disadvantaged being further disadvantaged. Even an analysis of our school holiday journeys showed that most of the candidates came from the "A" and "B" streams. It could not be a social class correlation in a school like Northcliffe, because nearly all of them came from the same socio-economic group.

It was not difficult in the circumstances to persuade the staff to move experimentally in the direction of unstreaming. We realised of course that different techniques would have to be adopted - small group and individual tuition would be the order of the day with mixed ability classes rather than class teaching - and our chalk and talk sessions would need drastic revision and pruning. We devoted two of our monthly staff meetings to this subject. Our staff conferences take place once a term. We decide in advance when the next monthly staff meeting shall be given over to some current educational problem. The Home Economics Department then provides tea for the staff, and we stay on for most of the evening to talk through our problems together. Sometimes we have outside speakers to give us some help and advice, but more often than not we prefer our own solutions.

Parents were informed of the changes we proposed to make, and the reasons behind them, at our subsequent half-termly parent-teachers' meetings, and whether it was that the changes we proposed were to be gradual, or whether the reasoning behind the move appealed to their sense of fairness, I do not know, but very little apprehension was expressed, and no disapproval whatsoever.

I suppose it took about six months for the effect of the first moderate move towards unstreaming - the broad banding - to become apparent. The pattern of behaviour became more even - approximating more to the "A" and "B" streams that we used to have than to

the former "C's" and "D's". There were still some classes which
behaved better than others - there always will be, I suppose - but the
clear distinction between the goodies and baddies seemed to be
disappearing. We were also retaining more of our Duke of Edinburgh
Awards candidates, although we still had a majority coming from
the more able band than from the other band. We discussed the
results of our changes at monthly staff meetings, and found general
agreement that we had improved the morale of the boys appreciably;
the standards of work were not suffering and many of them were
making more of an effort to show us that our trust was not misplaced. They understood what we were trying to do, of course,
because we had made it the subject of discussion in classes and after
morning assembly. The staff and I felt that we could move on to
complete unstreaming with the first year forms, and that a propitious
time to do it would occur when the Boys' and Girls' Schools were
due to combine in 1964. If we found then it was a success, we could
allow it to grow through the whole school, until in five years' time
the broad banding would have given place to a complete system of
mixed ability groupings.

We decided to rationalise the teaching of mixed ability groups even
to the extent of discontinuing class lists and rank orders altogether.
There would be no set piece examinations, but we would have
continuous individual assessment instead. With class lists and rank
orders, prizes would go as well. If you are fortunate enough to be
bright and intelligent and able to perform better than your fellows,
this is sufficient reward in itself. You will need no reinforcement of
your ego with a school prize. In any case monetary reward is likely
to follow you all the days of your life as a direct result of your
superior ability, and it is the effect on the others which we should
be tempering as much as possible. So we decided to use our prize
fund to pay for school journeys for those who otherwise might not
be able to afford to go on them. I have never noticed anyone working
less well because there was no prize forthcoming at the end of the
course.

Curriculum Reform

Just as we had revised our teaching methods to suit the needs of
mixed ability groups, so we began to feel the need for changes in our
subject teaching and our syllabuses. Individual development and

aptitude were not important to the old style syllabus writers. The subject was the important thing - Geography must be pursued as though everyone was destined to be a geographer, History as though we would all be historians. The specialists never allowed themselves or the pupils to cross the invisible barriers - an hour for History, an hour for Geography, an hour and a half for English. We all know the staff room strife that ensues if one specialist loses half an hour from his precious time allowance for the GCE syllabus - all is lost! The specialist will not have time to cram it all in. Sir Alec Clegg, our incomparable Education Officer in the West Riding, reckoned we were more interested in pot filling than fire lighting. But teachers in many quarters were beginning to question boldly, openly and irreverently the value of university imposed syllabuses, and some notice was being taken of their ribald criticism in the Schools' Council and later on quite a number of the CSE panels. We were coming to terms with the computers who were offering to store up all our reference material for us in their memory banks and save us from having to burn the midnight oil to do it ourselves. What we were left with was the need for wisdom to employ that stored up knowledge - the need for fire lighting. The whole emphasis was shifting from the accumulation of factual information toward individual selection and search for information relevant to problem solving.

In the West Riding of Yorkshire, Sir Alec Clegg and his team of advisory staff used Woolley Hall, with its splendid residential facilities, to provide an all the year round programme of in-service courses for West Riding teachers. The surroundings were so attractive and the social provision so considerate, that these courses were very popular with the teachers. Their influence upon the revolution in teaching methods which has occurred in the field of primary education towards child centred learning has been remarkable. Sir Alec always lamented the slowness of the Secondary schools to respond to the changes happening to children in these formative earlier years in the Junior schools, though he realised well enough that the nigger in the woodpile was the 16+ examination system. It was no accident therefore that he and many willing allies worked away at the CSE system to ensure that teachers would be as free to use Mode 3 continuous assessment on school based syllabuses as possible. That is why an analysis of CSE entries shows the largest field of Mode 3 syllabuses operating in Yorkshire. This had far reaching effects upon the Northcliffe School - as you might imagine.

For several years we had been experimenting with team-teaching and block timetabling in the practical subjects - the kids having two half days a week with either one or two members of the team in one or another of the Arts and Crafts - in the lower school on a rotation basis to give them a wide variety of experience, as they grew older on an optional basis so that they could have the opportunity of staying with something they enjoyed so much that they wanted real proficiency at it. We had some very good Mode 3 examination results in this area of education which was admirably suited to individual development. We felt satisfied that we were fulfilling the needs of the kids in ways which were more clearly to be seen than in other areas of their studies. Drama and Movement were other successful fields because of their response to individual needs. We decided that the time had come to rationalize the more traditional academic subjects into something more logical than the sheep-pen division of time and talent showing up on our timetables.

Ten of the staff had been to a Summer School course organised by the West Riding at Bretton Hall concerned with integrated studies and exploratory ways of learning. When they returned to school in September, I found myself playing the role of a slightly reactionary Headmaster besieged by a band of eager reformers all keen to change the curriculum immediately, if not sooner. I could even indulge in a little cautionary "take it easy boys" play acting which only served to make them more eager than ever to get something going. This was a very happy position for a Headmaster to be in, and I started acting as ways and means man straight away. The joy of the whole operation was that the staff concerned started holding their own conferences to plan what they wanted to do without any dragooning whatsoever from me.

So it came about that we started Humanities Projects - team-taught on a block time-table with the four forms of fourth year leavers in 1966. A great deal of the work took the boys and girls out of school on all sorts of visits into Yorkshire and Derbyshire - into the hills and dales and even as far as the coast round Flamborough Head. We spent a very considerable proportion of our capitation allowance on transporting them to interesting places, and we also found them quite willing to pay for much of it themselves. The enthusiasm of the team of teachers communicated itself to the kids in such fashion that the success of the venture was assured, and the enjoyment of the boys and girls was obvious.

It was almost a foregone conclusion that we should now proceed to adopt these methods with the children who came to us from the Junior schools, and allow this pattern to grow throughout the school. One of the great advantages of this decision was that the abrupt transition from Junior school to Secondary, so traumatic for many of the kids, would be made easier. They would stay with one teacher for at least ten periods of the week and be using methods of learning not unfamiliar to them from earlier practice. When we started in September 1967 with eight mixed ability forms of boys and girls, with teams of teachers - all volunteers for this scheme - block timetabled for ten periods of a thirty period week, we all felt that we had taken part in a successful revolution. The themes we had chosen were suitable to the age and interests of the first formers concerned, with plenty of meat on their bones to support investigation at individual level and give plenty of scope for the kids' own initiative and resource - Water, Inventions, Time, Woodlands, Birds and Animals, The Sea - with room for "mini" seasonal topics at Christmas and Easter thrown in. This gave us a very wide field of action. It was obvious that a topic like "The Sea" would be timed for June and July with a couple of visits to the coast as part of the excitement.

In the following three years, by September 1971, the new curriculum covered the activities of the first, second and third forms and the crucial time had arrived for its projection into the two years which were usually sacred to the preparation for examinations - we were poised on the threshold, and with a very heavy responsibility to the kids for the future. What could we do to make it possible to pursue methods which were making good sense to us as well as to the boys and girls, and at the same time offer them a chance of proper certification at the end of the next two years? The Schools Council and the NUT had both appealed for the introduction of a single leaving exam - so we pre-empted this development by asking both the CSE and the GCE Boards to accept a Humanities syllabus for Mode 3 continuous assessment over a two year period for separate certification in the four component disciplines concerned - English

Language, Geography, History and Moral Studies. We formulated a syllabus with the help of the Stenhouse Projects published for the Schools Council, the integrated "O" level syllabus accepted by the AEB from the Hedley Walter School at Brentwood, the Humanities syllabus put to the CSE Board by Rossington Comprehensive School, with whom we have established links, and material of our furnishing. The object of including an appreciable amount of already accepted syllabus material was to ensure as wide a recognition for boys and girls gaining certificates as possible, as well as to be able to identify ourselves with like minded schools for purposes of assessment and to be sure of a plentiful supply of teaching resources. There followed a series of top level meetings with the Boards concerned. Agreement was reached and our courses were started.

This was a logical step to take with mixed ability groups and we could continue our Humanities Projects without having recourse to unnatural divisions between examination and non examination candidates. The boys and girls could still progress at their own level of ability. At the same time some further flexibility was possible through the alternative courses which we intended to offer to any who wanted to work right outside the system.

We had broken fresh ground with the methods of assessment which the two Boards had agreed upon. We found the "O" level GCE committee surprisingly open minded about what we were attempting to do, and willing to spend a great deal of time discussing the fairest means of operating continuous assessment techniques to avoid limiting the boys' and girls' fields of research as much as possible. In the examination we now give sixty per cent of the marks for course work, twenty per cent for the final dissertations - the boys and girls choosing their titles from areas connected with their research over the past two years. One dissertation is submitted for each of the four disciplines involved. They are written under classroom conditions with careful supervision. The boys and girls can bring in reference books and material, but must acknowledge quotations. There is no strict limit on the time allowed - they can take all day if necessary. The remaining twenty per cent of the marks goes for their conversational ability to communicate ideas concerning the work they have chosen to do. What a change from the days when we were asked to answer quite involved questions about, for instance, Shakespeare's plays without the script of the play in front of us.

What drama critic writing an informed article for a serious journal would do a thing like that? It has been a joy to me to see the kids arriving on the days appointed for the writing of their dissertations carrying materials they have found to help them to write something worthwhile on the subject - completely relaxed and ready to admit that they quite enjoy the exercise.

Perhaps I am taking for granted that the direct connection between teaching mixed ability groups and the changes we have made in the curriculum is apparent and logical. We find that the broad themes we are working on have a universal interest for kids of any ability, and there are sufficient resources available to sustain research at all levels. One of the criticisms one hears from teachers about the "Stenhouse" projects is that they are more suitable for sixth formers or students than for fifteen or sixteen year olds. They have missed the point, I think. They are, indeed, adult topics of universal interest. At what level you pursue discussion rests, however, with the teacher and the group concerned. Relations between the Sexes, War and Society, Education, The Family, The Community in which We Live, The Preservation of Our Environment are some of the themes which we find sustain a great deal of interest, and the boys and girls can choose either one or two themes of their own to work on in the last term before their final assessment is made.

There are still some areas of the curriculum at Northcliffe where unstreaming and mixed ability grouping are not adhered to completely. The Maths Department adopts setting within their block timetable allocation, and so upsets the pattern somewhat. We have discussed this on more than one occasion, but can only agree on a compromise that it should be very broad setting rather than an absolute "ABCD" division. The Modern Languages Department also functions with groups in the upper school who opt to learn a foreign language, and this results in groups that are plainly not of mixed ability. These deviations from the pattern are not sufficiently great to upset the social well-being of our boys and girls and cause them to feel graded - or as I think they felt in the old system - degraded.

Since I have been asked to write this case study of Northcliffe, perhaps I might be permitted to look into the future a little way. Does it make sense to divide adolescents at various stages of maturity by age groups? Certainly it makes for easy administration, but it is hardly true to life. When I consider what used to happen in some of the best of our village schools, and the civilised behaviour which came out of the small all-age mixed ability groups to be found in them, it makes me wonder what strengths we are wasting. There is still plenty of room for worthwhile development in not only mixed ability grouping, but mixed age grouping as well. If we do this, we shall have stopped interfering with the natural order of things to such an extent that we shall discover normal relationships in schools becoming the rule rather than the exception.

Chapter 2
Fairlop Secondary Girls' School

M.R. Horne

Fairlop Secondary Girls' School was built in 1935 on the north eastern side of the Essex town of Ilford. The school was originally administered as an excepted district of Essex but now falls within the boundaries of the London Borough of Redbridge.

The plans for comprehensivisation of the Secondary schools in the Borough have suffered many setbacks so that reorganisation has not yet fully taken place. Particularly relevant to the Fairlop situation is the fact that our school remains still Secondary Modern whilst only a few miles away stand reorganised Comprehensives. To maintain a reputation for being a worthwhile school offering plenty of scope for bright pupils in face of the more attractive facilities offered by larger and better endowed local Comprehensives becomes harder each day. The strain of such a situation must affect one's attitude to experimental courses and innovatory practices.

Having painted this rather gloomy backdrop let us proceed to look at the school itself. It is a building of redbrick and large rectangular wood-framed windows - the external elevation derives rather heavily from what might be termed bastard Georgian - designs much used by Essex architects in the 1930s - respectable, solid and built to last.

By inference therefore resistant to change! The internal accommodation was identical on both upper and lower floors - eight classrooms apiece, two practical rooms, one laboratory, hall, cloaks, staff accommodation, a few built-in cupboards. Over the years the lower floor of the school has been handed over from boys, to boys and girls and finally to girls only. Internally, some rooms have been put together with intervening walls removed, with stock cupboards built into such enlarged rooms. Cloakrooms have become division rooms, clothes are hung on pegs in the corridors, a cupboard has become the Deputy Head's room, an art technician's room, a music practice room etc. etc. Any school that works with less than enough teaching bases will recognise these kinds of transformation! The most imaginative translation apart from these described has been the adaptation of the concrete corridor that runs beside the arts room as a work and discussion area with carpeted floor and display surfaces on walls. Demountable classrooms stand in the small school grounds around the main school building. The particularly solid and traditional design of the main building has been one of the difficulties when one has tried to reshape the curriculum. However, in spite of this, curriculum changes were made as we all realised that if we were to wait for the perfect or even a helpful building we should wait forever.

Modest, but radical, alterations began in our organisation in 1965 as a result of Pilot Course No. 1 held at Goldsmiths' College under the leadership of Mrs. Charity James. The Curriculum Laboratory that Mrs. James led and the literature that the laboratory published greatly influenced the Fairlop staff since the Head and five or six staff members were seconded in turn for a term each to participate in its courses. The value of being closely connected with the Education Department of a College or Institute cannot be overstated, as one's knowledge of current Education Theory is tested and contested constantly as soon as one breaks away from the accepted modes of learning in Secondary school.

The manner of change-making in our school followed this pattern. Teachers dissatisfied with working in a streamed situation were invited, regardless of subject taught, to express their dissatisfaction and to offer to plan a new first year curriculum which would be presented to our ninety eleven year old pupils on entry to the school. The volunteers were enthusiastic in their willingness and planned an interdisciplinary programme for the new girls that covered about fifty per cent of the week. The remainder of the time was devoted to the more traditional teaching of subjects that we felt could not be handled in a thematic fashion. Such subjects, we decided, were Mathematics, French, Physical Education and later Science and Domestic Science. The choice of the first three subjects named seems now with hindsight to be quite a common one found in many schools but in our planning days of 1965 there was no-one to consult who had any experience. Science and Domestic Science I find integrate quite well in other schools but not particularly well at Fairlop.

With this decision made, we had by subtraction a list of subjects that the first year team must cover - all the other specialist disciplines in the ordinary Secondary timetable. We selected from amongst our volunteer experimenters the five most able to be adequate teachers of the Expressive Arts, English and the Humanities - in the Fairlop case History, Geography, Sociology, R.E. We felt we were thereby making a valuable bridge for our pupils from the generally-speaking class-centred education of the Primary school to the more fragmented specialist programme of the traditional Secondary school.

Having determined the subjects they were to teach, the staff then got down to the really interesting matter of how they were going to do it. What an opportunity for ideals and hopes to be allowed full rein of expression! The term of planning was an exciting one and optimism knew no bounds. The first piece of organisation to be scrapped was, by mutual consent, streaming. The inhumanity, the inaccuracy, the self-fulfilling prophecy of it all! How glad we were to have reasons to discard it and how many reasons we found! I still find, nine hard years later, that I believe all those reasons we expressed and would not choose to teach in a streamed school again. The optimism and self-confidence of the pupils when free of these absurd cyphers "ABCD" is a pleasure to see. Careers as opposed to jobs, job-satisfaction as opposed to salary size alone, day release or further full-time education are now natural demands from our leavers - an overwhelming proof for us teachers, if we needed encouragement, of the success of our early experiments.

Undoing the first key shackle - streaming - freed us for our subsequent more flexible organisations. If the first year pupils were no longer 1A,

1B, 1C, but four mixed ability groups, the year group could be treated as a whole with a common curriculum with common staff for all. We began to talk about year groups rather than forms 1A, 1B, 1C and eventually, some years later, arranged to expend some of our scale points on year group tutors.

The second most important move was that from a three-form entry school where lessons were given to the three forms by three staff at any one time to the more intimate arrangements of three forms divided into four teaching groups. The smaller teaching group enabled us to provide a more relaxed atmosphere and a more personal approach to teaching. It seemed essential if teachers were to give up "class teaching" and offer instead discussion, group work and activity that the number of pupils they were dealing with would be reduced from thirty to twenty-three or so. The first move by the original IDE* team in 1965 is perpetuated still and staff would be reluctant now to revert to the former arrangements. The obvious concomitant of smaller classes is however fewer periods of the week for marking and preparation by staff. The quality of marking has certainly dropped as a result of increased pupil-contact hours but I would consider the value of smaller classes far outweighed this disadvantage.

Each form group is composed, on entry, of pupils of every level of ability from the brightest to the dullest. We arrive at these form groups by information from Primary school record cards and by visits to the Primary school in June and July by our first year tutor and as many teachers as we can spare. At the same time as we organise a spread of ability for each group, we also arrange for every girl to be with at least one friend. We draw from about ten contributory schools and there will automatically be many "strangers" in the newly composed forms. It seems helpful and reassuring that familiar faces shall also be found.

For our pupils these two changes into smaller and unstreamed groups seemed pure advantage but we had not reckoned with the wrath of a few parents whose children would have been "A" but who now were unlabelled. They sorely missed the gratification that they were denied by our so-hopeful new arrangements and they raised long and vigorous protests that would have daunted all but a very committed

---

* Interdisciplinary Enquiry.

team of teachers. Misgivings and forebodings were uttered and, had not the pupils in the main been happy to come to school, we should have lost many girls to the more formal neighbouring schools. Five years later improved examination results told their own story and our methods were proven effective, if not yet popular with our parents. The continuance of unstreaming and informal teaching was made possible by the enthusiastic efforts of the first IDE teacher team who "sold" their system successively year after year to their colleagues, so that after five years the transition was complete. It cannot be over-emphasised that volunteers are essential to the success of any change. Enthusiastic pioneers add initial success which subsequent lesser enthusiasts cannot usually maintain. Sceptical saboteurs can quickly undermine the morale and confidence of experimenters.

During the transition period 1965-1970 it became obvious that our school examination system would need complete overhaul. It had been the custom in the earlier streamed school to enter about fifteen of the brighter pupils (11+ failures and borderline candidates as they were) for a limited number of "O" levels. The remainder of the year group was entered for a school examination and given a private school leaving certificate. We were often wrong in our diagnosis of who should and who should not take "O" Level. Also surprisingly good results, because of excellent motivation discovered very late in Secondary school life, were quite often found in the non "O" Level pupils. One such pupil, still a close friend, brings her own pupils to visit us regularly on a sociological practical excursion from an ILEA Comprehensive. When I think how we labelled this person a "B" in her eleventh year I shudder at the nonsense of it all. Fairlop was obviously going to need examination that fitted its own practical, active, non-streamed self and fortunately CSE Mode 3 was there for the using, providing of course that there were teachers capable of writing and proving the worth of alternative syllabuses. Fortunately we have always attracted an abundance of such talent amongst our teaching staff and the considerable working task was undertaken, submitted and accepted. Our own struggles are of no particular interest but the general point indicated here is that the examinations used must reflect the education provided. It would be an unsatis-factory school indeed that altered its teaching methods in the first three years and then in years four and five suddenly back-pedalled

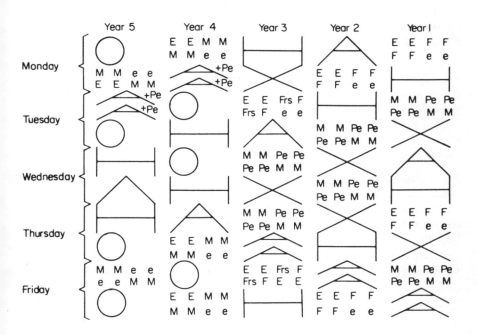

Proposed Timetable Allocation 1973-4

Key
H = Humanities (History, Geography, Sociology, Religious Education)
E = English
M = Mathematics
O = Main options
X = Science (General Science, Home Economics)
F = French
A = Arts (Art, Music, Movement, Drama, English)
Frs = French Studies
PE = Physical Education (see also Movement)
Needlecrafts occur within Home Economics or within Arts.

and started cramming furiously in a traditional way to enter its
students for a traditional examination. As a sample of our use this
year, 1974, of the CSE examinations, a list follows of our entries:-

Art and Craft; Commerce; Home Economics; English; Geography;
History; Mathematics; French; Music; Art of Movement; Needlecraft;
Religious Education; Biology; Chemistry; Elementary Sociology.

In the above paragraphs I hope I have traced the path of change in
Fairlop from a streamed subject-based school to an interdisciplinary,
unstreamed school. We have had dozens of timetables in those nine
years - our current one is shown above - a remarkably simple affair
with a simplicity that comes after years of honing and refining all
the awkwardnesses. I even believe we may be able to use it again -
an unexpected bonus that has never occurred before.

To expand the Fairlop timetable, the explanation of a sample
situation may serve to illustrate. For instance the letter "H" denotes
Humanities. For our purposes we use this word to describe the
subjects History, Geography, Sociology and Religious Education in
the first three years of the school. Four specialists form a team and
they will all be working simultaneously in the same age group. If they
wish to give a lecture to start the session and follow it up with worksheets in the four subjects, the timetable allows this. If they each
wish to teach for one lesson one class in the year group, the timetable
will also allow it. If an outside speaker is to address the year group he
can easily be accommodated - similarly educational visits can be
arranged for the half day without any other subject teacher being
inconvenienced.

The advantages of this flexible arrangement, only possible because of
mixed ability grouping for a common curriculum, are very obvious.
It is a positive encouragement to any group of staff who wish to
write a thematic syllabus. The most recent example of the use of this
was when I saw a year group working on the theme of "Wealth/
Poverty". The History syllabus was a fairly straightforward chronological story of the British attitude to poverty and wealth over the
past few centuries, with emphasis on the church assumption of
responsibility for the poor followed by state responsibility. The
geographical syllabus dealt with areas of the world with natural
resources and the development of trade. The Sociology teacher used
the local environment in which to find examples of poverty and

wealth and took discussion lessons on deprivation, human needs, family life, environmental hardship and so forth. The R.E. teacher gave lessons on the holy poverty ideas that St. Francis and other saints and ascetics have exemplified.

Besides finding a rich vein of information that lies well within the heart of History or Geography, an interdisciplinary method teacher realises that one of the excitements of teaching in this way is that the areas that fall between say History and Geography or History and Sociology provide many other less well worn fields of enquiry. Thus the use of block timetabling is, we find, very helpful to our school in that it enlivens our syllabuses.

The manner in which the Arts team (labelled "A") makes use of its block of time is different, as one would expect. I find that its ways of using the situation exploit the possibilities of block time-tabling to its limit. The specialists who form an "A" team are Music, Art, Dance, Drama and English teachers. All being concerned with the expressive arts, they share a common belief in the need for rich stimuli to provoke a creative response. It will be easily understood by staff who teach those subjects how helpful it is to work with the resources of a team whose ideas can be shared. The preparation sessions in which team members pool their random thoughts are the most exciting sort of staff meeting at which I have ever been present. We have had dozens of such meetings at Fairlop and found them a suitable occasion at which we could welcome our numerous guests. The witnessing of the staff at work in such a session gives insight into the school's philosophy. A later walk around the school is we hope more meaningful with this preamble.

How do we evaluate our curriculum changes - unstreaming, block timetabling, subject integration, Mode 3 CSE, use of the local community - the local environment is our "open" school. Opinions vary as to our success or failure. Perhaps it would be fair to choose a very old and reputable yardstick as a measuring device, - not an instrument that we would wish to choose, as in our book, examina-tions are not the be all and end all. But examination success ranks high as a criterion of respectability. Here are a few facts:

1966 1 or 2 pupils to further education

1973 26 pupils to further education

1974 probably 45

Single subject examination entries:

1968 — 186

1971 — 321

1974 — 533

Although the normal five twelfths (about forty of the age group) could have left school at Easter 1974 only six pupils did in fact leave. The remainder have all taken CSE examinations Mode 3. The average number of subjects per candidate is 5.5.

It seems as though the school's refusal to label some pupils "A" and others "D" has resulted in raising the confidence of all in their ability to be examined. Also the non-competitive approach to learning has obviously created a greater number of "students" who regard education as something one goes on seeking regardless of age. There is certainly an aggressive demand for more from the pupils of our school. The staff would regard such a demand as the reward for their innovatory labours.

Chapter 3
Vauxhall Manor School

E.M. Hoyles

Vauxhall Manor School was formed in 1957 by the amalgamation of a Secondary Modern school with a Central school. From the beginning it worked in mixed ability groups since its Head Teacher believed, as did many others of the Heads of the new London Comprehensive Schools, that to continue the tripartite system under one roof was undesirable. Although this feeling of idealism persisted for some time, the problems arising from mixed ability teaching and the need to establish the new Comprehensive schools and give them parity of esteem, especially at the level of public examination results with the existing Grammar schools, caused many Head Teachers to change from mixed ability grouping into streaming and later into broad-banding. However, so far as Vauxhall Manor was concerned, the idea of mixed ability grouping was never dropped.

The school was housed in old buildings on two sites to which some adaptations were made, but, inevitably, it was not able to provide the kind of accommodation possible in a purpose built building and later, as time went by and the intake grew, the problems of over-crowding became quite serious. In addition there was always, as in other London schools, the problem of providing sufficient playing space and this has remained a difficulty to the present time.

As is the case in most other inner city schools, the problems of the intake were considerable. At the beginning, the school drew from a very mixed population of wide social backgrounds but, as time went on and with the change in inner city population, the emphasis has come increasingly to be on lower ability children and the school has the same problems as other London schools of children who have difficulties in literacy and numeracy. There are also grave social problems in the district and these are bound to be reflected in children's attitudes and behaviour in school itself.

As time went by, the problems of grouping became more difficult. Originally it had been decided to group the children according to their date of birth so that it was possible to find in one class children of September/October birth dates and in another class children of July/August birth dates. These last children, who always face difficulties because of their shortened Primary School experience, were still at a disadvantage when they came into the Secondary school and, as time went by, began to be considered as "the less able group". In addition, the children in the classes that contained the September/October/November birth dates were under serious pressure from their peers when reaching statutory leaving age and there were always considerable problems for those who were able to stay on but who felt themselves required by their group to leave school and to start work.

The whole question of grouping, therefore, came into reconsideration because of this situation. Eventually, it was decided that perhaps a fairer way might be to arrange classes according to the initial letter of the child's surname, arranging the entrants in alphabetical order and dividing them up into eight classes. This system had the advantage of showing the children that they had been put into classes for reasons that had nothing to do with their own ability, whether based on intelligence tests or on academic achievement in the Junior school. It is also the case that in an eight-form entry school such an arrangement is statistically likely to provide equal classes of widely mixed ability. This does not mean, however, that all the classes are of equal social mix, nor does it mean that every class is exactly the same, because without fail, year after year, there have been classes that have been more difficult to deal with than others, classes that have been more fragmented, and on the other hand classes that have more quickly settled down into a composite whole.

It seems likely, therefore, that there is always a necessity to find some way, perhaps during the course of the first half-year, of doing some regrouping in order to spread the opportunities available to all pupils over the full range, since it is possible, if classes that are difficult remain together, that they will, in fact, benefit very little from all that is offered them in the school.

One is faced, therefore, with eight classes in each year all of whom are of equal mix and ability so that there is no reason why they cannot all have exactly the same curriculum. It was to the curriculum that we turned our major thinking.

In our consideration of the curriculum at Vauxhall Manor School we had to bear in mind the problems that were inherent in the school situation for many of the children who came to us. These were children who had, for many years, been faced with the idea of failure, who had found it impossible to succeed in great areas of their school work and who had been considered to be unsuitable for the more advanced, and therefore more desirable, forms of education. Since the opportunities for all to be successful in some area were what we were trying to provide, it was necessary to think of a very wide curriculum and this is what we set ourselves to do. On the other hand, since there was no division between the classes on the grounds of ability, there was no reason at all to make any parts of the curriculum the sole prerogative of any particular groups, nor was there any possibility of thinking that the most able should have little experience of practical work since, as all classes were equally mixed, the same opportunities had to be available to all.

Such a system gives considerable opportunities for children who are late developers, as many of ours are bound to be. There are also opportunities for children whose early years in school have been disturbed, either by home and social problems or by personal problems like poor health. These form a sizeable proportion of our population and therefore opportunities for them would be especially welcome. In addition, there were many children in our school who had difficulty in learning and who learnt at a very slow rate. The opportunities for them of the common curriculum were extremely great.

We have in fact delayed specialisation until quite late, making the major choice at the end of the fourth year, instead of, as is traditional, at the end of the third year. This inevitably raises problems of a different kind since the demands of specialisation have to be met in some way and the problems also that are raised by the external examinations system, which is still largely traditional, had to be overcome by a careful consideration of the amount of time available. Our system, therefore, means that from years one to four, with very few exceptions such as a second language and the special science subjects, pupils follow a common curriculum, whilst in the fifth year they will follow a limited number of subjects at greater depth.

Unfortunately, whatever system one uses, the amount of time available to the pupil in school remains the same and the demands on the pupils' time are very great. It is, therefore, important to look at each moment of the school day to see that the greatest use is being made of this. Better use can actually be made of class time and this we came to consider as we thought about the whole question of classroom organisation and the pupil's role, but obviously there is a great saving to be made if subjects can be combined, the teachers reinforcing one another and enhancing the pupils' understanding of the subjects concerned. A move towards integrated work or at the very least combined and co-ordinated work was, therefore, of major importance.

Far from solving all problems, the introduction of a common curriculum for so long in school is bound to raise others. For example, if one is not going to introduce choice until quite late, is one in fact depriving a number of pupils? If a curriculum is going to be wide as well as common, are we assuming that all pupils are able equally to manage all subjects? Do we force ourselves into a curriculum "straight-jacket"? On the other hand, it is quite clear that where children are asked to make choices at an early age, they may frequently be ill-equipped to do this and, whilst being able to make a positive choice, may often be unaware of the consequences of the rejection of subjects they have not chosen. The final difficulty, of course, is how to deal with subjects that have traditionally been accepted as being suitable for the most able only. This can include the Science subjects; it also includes Modern Languages, and therefore, following hard upon a consideration of the curriculum, comes the whole question of the syllabus itself.

Very little research work has been done on the syllabus in the school and yet it is perhaps one of the most important documents upon which schools rely. In the traditional setting, the syllabus can often contain the exact amount of work that must be covered during the course of each school year and dependent upon this is the question of pupils being entered, or not, for examinations. At one time it was possible for the Head of a Department to expect that every piece of work could be noted in the syllabus and the amount of the textbook to be covered could also be stipulated there. Today, with greater diversity in our schools, such an expectation is not likely but, nevertheless, there must be clear thinking about the part a syllabus plays, since for many young teachers it is a form of in-service training that must not be neglected. It is obvious that some boundaries must be drawn to indicate what the pupils must have covered during the course of a year and there should be a clear indication of what must follow the present year so that the teacher can be aware of what areas are to be covered in future.

We have tried syllabuses of different kinds, some indicating the maximum/minimum amount to be covered during the course of a year, others indicating that the subject will be covered either in shallow terms by the least able and in terms of greater depth by the most able, or arranged in periods of time so that some children during the space of a month will cover considerable amounts of work on a particular theme, whilst others will cover smaller amounts but still enough to give them an adequate grounding for a teacher in the following year to go still further. It is possible to think in terms of themes that must be covered by children during the course of a period of time whilst yet other teachers will think in terms of children acquiring particular skills which can be developed later.

On one occasion, we experimented with an on-going syllabus, children starting at the same point at the beginning of the first year and going on at their own pace for as long as the teacher was able to remain with them. It was quite obvious that some children in a short space of time could cover considerable amounts of work, especially if they were allowed unhampered progress. Others went very much more slowly than one would have expected. Unfortunately, the teacher concerned was not able to stay in the school for more than about eighteen months and the difficulties that faced a teacher taking up the work at a later time were immense. As a result, this system was not continued, but it obviously contains the germs of something that could be a very useful development.

Amongst the things that Heads of Departments deal with in devising their syllabuses come first of all the aims of the subject and its place in the total school philosophy, the areas of study that the subject is going to encompass, the lines upon which it is possible for the subject to develop, particularly in relation to the different years, the various teaching methods that can be used, different forms of classroom organisation, the resources that are available to the teacher, where they may be found and some indication of how they can be used, the methods of assessment used in the Department, the ways of recording the pupils' work and giving some indication of the progress of each pupil, how reports can be made up and the place of visits in the Department. The syllabus may well include information about parallel work done in different Departments and some indication of how integration or co-ordination may take place. There is usually some indication too of what is available for the Department in the library and usually a calendar of events, including dates of Departmental meetings and indications of what the school will require at different periods of the school year. These will include things like Open Evenings, Parents' Meetings, dates for school reports, external examinations and so on.

Clearly, the most important part of mixed ability teaching takes place in the classroom. It is in the classroom, by virtue of the teacher's attitude and the pupils' attitudes, that the success or failure of the system will depend. Obviously then, a school must spend a good deal of time talking about classroom organisation and finding ways to develop this so that it is adequate to the requirements that are placed upon it.

So far as Vauxhall Manor is concerned, the physical provision of classrooms is what one would expect to find in an old three-decker building. The classrooms are large and airy but they are high and they are noisy because of the brickwork and the fact that they are usually off halls or large corridors that are used for movement. Because there is very little space other than the classrooms in the school, most of the work that is done must take place within them. There is little opportunity for allocating small areas for discussion or small rooms for recording, and everything has to take place inside the classrooms themselves. We have tried to have the classrooms furnished with tables and chairs in order to make group work more easy. This means that storage must be provided for the pupils by means of lockers and, because there are so many resources required, there must be a good deal of cupboard space. On the other hand, many activities will be practical and it is necessary to have work-tops of various kinds available on which the children can paint or draw or model. Similarly there must be room inside the classroom for showing films or film strips and provision must be made for this as well. Ideally, each classroom should have running water but this is not always possible to achieve.

So far as resources are concerned there will, of course, be books of various kinds. We seldom rely on sets of class textbooks but prefer to have groups of different books, sometimes shared out amongst several classes. There will be reference books and a small class library. There will be assignment cards and worksheets and a good deal of material for reference. The organisation of this and its cataloguing are probably among the most difficult tasks a Department has to undertake and we have found ourselves in the past in the situation where there was a considerable amount of material but access to it was very difficult, either because the cataloguing was inefficient or because the storage of it meant that it was not possible for people to get to it easily.

In addition to these resources, which are steadily built up over the years and can be the result of teachers working together, as will be explained later, the school has for a very long time steadily built up its audio-visual resources. We use tape recorders, record players, film-strip projectors, film loop projectors, overhead projectors, all of which are quite common in our classrooms. It is essential for pupils, as well as teachers, to be able to use these and this must form part of the pupils' training. For many years the teachers themselves organised these resources, but fortunately over the past four or five years it has been possible to have in the school a Media Resources Officer whose task is to look after the equipment and, most particularly, to instruct teachers in its use and in its developing use. The running of courses and the granting of certificates for teachers have meant a considerable increase in their versatility in the class-room itself. We are moving now to the training of pupils in this matter and the awarding of certificates to them as they attain proficiency in using the various pieces of equipment.

It is important to remember that all the resources that are made available inside the classroom will be provided by the teacher and will be chosen by her in order to give her pupils more learning opportunities. Where the teacher has no wish for a pupil to be doing any particular thing, then obviously the provision of that item will not be made. What use the pupils make of the resources will depend upon them and there is no limitation on this, but it is important to remember that it is upon the teacher that the organisation initially depends and the provision of resources will be her major responsibility. Clearly, to select the resources that will be provided, the teacher needs to be a specialist and it is quite obvious from every point of view that mixed ability teaching requires teachers of the highest professional calibre.

The classroom structure is now becoming clear. It is much more a workshop than a place of instruction. It may frequently look untidy and it is quite clear that many different kinds of activity may go on inside it. It is not a place where pupils can rely on one method of instruction only and there is no reason why desks should always face one way, or why the teacher should be the focal point. However, it would be foolish to assume that all lessons are taught in an informal way, since there will be many reasons why the teacher will want to have a class lesson or will want to have the pupils facing her, perhaps every time they are in the classroom with her.

Since there are so many opportunities inside the classroom, it is obvious that the teacher will need to group her pupils in different ways and this has to be most carefully considered since it is often a point of accusation that inside the classroom the pupils will be streamed into different groups. Whilst it is true that there will be occasions where the teacher may require pupils of similar abilities to work together for particular ends, it will not be necessary to do this consistently. On the other hand, there is a good deal to be said for flexibility of groups, groups that are sometimes chosen by the teacher, sometimes by the pupils themselves, sometimes forming almost haphazardly according to the pupils' interests. Clearly such ways of working are not possible unless the children have a degree of self-confidence in their ability to handle this situation and have gained some expertise over the years as to how to make the best use of what is offered here so that the role of the pupil is a point that has to be considered most carefully.

Inside this kind of classroom the teacher has to provide for all ranges of ability, including the very slow learning child and the very bright child. All must have their opportunity to make the most of their particular talents and to better their own performances from lesson to lesson. The question of the remedial pupil is one that we have tried to tackle at Vauxhall Manor by a system of withdrawals. Over the years it has become obvious that standards of reading are lower than they should be and there will be many children coming into Secondary schools whose levels of ability in reading are much below what is required, especially for this method of working. Such children can be withdrawn in very small groups of four or five for special help from time to time. On the other hand, if there is a good deal of integrated or co-ordinated work between Departments, then the remedial teacher can work alongside these large groups in order to provide extra help for children who need it.

Equal care has to be taken over the bright child since there is always a temptation for the bright child to work at a slower pace in order to avoid standing out from her peers. Obviously the teacher's ability to deal with this situation cannot be confined solely to the lesson situation and has to depend upon the contact that is made with pupils at different times and the general attitude prevailing in the school. If a pupil is afraid to stand out from others then obviously something is seriously wrong and the whole attitude of the class must be looked at again.

The teacher is in this situation not the sole provider of information, as is often the case in the streamed situation. However, the teacher is the only professional in the classroom and it is upon her organisation and her teaching skill and professionalism that the pupils' progress will largely depend. It is clear from what was said earlier that all the material that is provided has been provided by her, but the use that is made of this depends upon the pupils themselves. The teacher, therefore, after having made provision, now moves into the role of senior tutor or guide, rather than simply that of instructor. Clearly a good deal of the teacher's work will be done outside the classroom and care must be taken to ensure that the preparation that is necessary for classes of mixed ability is adequately done.

Many people feel strongly that adequate provision cannot be made without excessive demands upon the teachers' time and a way must be found of dealing with this problem. We have found that where Departments work together to produce material that is suitable for a whole year or for different groups of pupils, then considerable benefits can come. Similarly, where teachers are working together across Departments, it is possible for material to be provided that can be dealt with in several different lessons.

One thing we found essential was to provide sufficient reprographic aids. There are many sophisticated instruments on the market and we felt that to use the money for the provision of these was as useful as providing money for large numbers of textbooks. Over the years, Departments will build up considerable banks of material, some of which can be provided by the pupils themselves as time goes on. These can be processed and refined so that there is a good deal available for the in-coming teacher to use, until she is sufficiently experienced to be able to devise her own.

One of the biggest difficulties is to provide materials that are comparable with the commercially produced material that pupils are used to, since to present pupils with a badly duplicated sheet containing inadequate information, will be to encourage from the pupils badly produced work of an inadequate standard too.

Inside the classroom, the teacher will be directing the pupils' work, will be ensuring that resources and materials are available and easily found, will be arranging groups, encouraging pupils to continue their work or to go further, prodding those who are slow or self-satisfied, stimulating those who are at a loss or who are engaged on unprofitable work, making quite certain the pupils are working together in a reasonable fashion and that the resources they bring to the lesson are being spread around so that all can benefit from them. In theory, the teacher should be able to stand back from the class a little to assess what progress is being made and to ensure that all are actively engaged. In practice the teacher may often find herself moving from group to group attempting to ensure that all are working adequately, sometimes varying the approach by having whole class sessions, sometimes ensuring that individual pupils are provided with opportunities outside the classroom by additional practical work, in visits to the library, moving into other Departments - all this requires supervision too.

Unless the teacher has taken pains over the training of pupils, there will be an intolerable burden not only of marking but also of recording and assessing - this must be adequately dealt with too. Clearly, to be able to deal with this kind of situation the teacher must, as I have already said, be a specialist and a highly trained professional teacher, but obviously since the school must depend on a large number of in-coming teachers inexperienced and still lacking in confidence, the school needs to mount a considerable in-service training programme.

Some of this will be done through Departments, some of it will be done by means of workshops and staff meetings and some of it will be undertaken by senior members of staff. Obviously we are well aware that what we have been able to do has not been enough. Many teachers have not been able to succeed adequately and have not found themselves getting the satisfaction that should come from such a rewarding job. There is a good deal of reading to be done also, and the teacher must gain other skills besides those that were developed in training in order to do the job efficiently. It is obvious in this situation that the teacher cannot repeat one year's experience again and again but must constantly be learning and expanding skills in order to deal with new situations and help children to develop still further.

Probably the most important aspect of this work is that it requires the pupil also to be adequately trained to help with her own education. Unless this is done from an early age the pupil will not be able to make the best use of the resources and the opportunities provided inside the classroom.

We have tried to undertake this training in a systematic way. Obviously, each Head of Department must indicate in the subject syllabus the way in which teachers are to ensure adequate pupil induction into the learning methods in her Department and each teacher will take pains to ensure that her pupils know what is expected of them in classroom techniques so that time is not wasted or pupils' confidence sapped by uncertainty over procedure. In addition, each pupil must understand through guidance and training the organisation of materials and of work in the room. Directions must be given over the recording of work which in the early stages should be a simple indication of what has been done. The teacher's checking of this will show whether enough work has been done or whether the pupil is working at too shallow a level; it will also stop any tendency to overstate the case. Early training must be done in assessment of work so that the pupil has clear goals to aim at when endeavouring to improve standards. We have tried a system called "Research Methods" for a specified time with each first year form in which pupils learned to use book-index and points of reference, beginning to learn how to skim etc. and then to use a dictionary, an encyclopaedia and other books of reference. It was important to teach them how to begin a project and how to illustrate it effectively and neatly. An equally important aspect was to learn how to discuss with other children points of value since the use of human resources in the classroom and the school and the acquisition of adequate social tools to make this possible needs teaching from the beginning. It is this easy human intercourse and readiness to give to others that make mixed ability schools the attractive places with high human values that they are. It cannot be too often emphasized however, that this does not happen by chance but is the result of thought, care and constant endeavour.

The library has already been dealt with but obviously its proper use is something that is learnt only over a period of months. There are other areas that can be used - different specialist libraries and the resources available in other places in the school; all these a child has to learn to use as well. Then there is her own locality, the local library, places of reference like the Town Hall; all these she needs to learn to use. She will also need to learn how to use people in the community, how to approach them, how to ask questions, how to organise the material that is obtained from them and, in particular, the courteous way of thanking people when once the material has been obtained. This will include the use of letter writing for information to be obtained from a distance.

A large part of the classroom organisation consists of various aids and from an early time the child has to learn how to use the tape recorder, the film strip projector, the film loop, the television and so on and obviously, as time goes on, it will be important for the child to be able to make her own programmes. In this case, we have found that our Media Resources Officer has been invaluable in giving the supplementary aid that a teacher will not have time to give.

A very important part of the child's training will be learning how to assess her achievements, not only against her own performance, but against the performance of others in the class, without this turning into a competitive activity. The acquisition of judgement in assessing performance is of extreme importance and when once this has been developed, it is possible to continue it as time goes on. It is important that it should be adequately dealt with by training right up into the sixth form. At a very early age a child has to record what has been done. Clearly, from the beginning it will be necessary for the teacher to check on this. In addition to recording the pupil will need to report on her own work because it is an important feature of the mixed ability class that the resources that each pupil is able to provide are relevant to the development of the remainder and a form of reporting on one's own achievement is of very great importance in this.

One of the main features of mixed ability classroom organisation is the numerous occasions on which children need to work in groups. The child has to learn to use the group activity effectively from the beginning. First of all, she needs to learn how to play her own part in the group. Sometimes she will be the leader of the group, directing others, at other times she will be a member working at someone else's direction; sometimes she will be working with the group, sometimes she will be working away from the group. In addition, she will need to grow in judgement of other people's ability and this can join the general teaching the school provides in respect for other people because, from an early stage, she will have to learn how to use other people's talents, not only for her own development but for the development of the group. It is important for her to learn how to apportion work to other members of the group so that when she becomes a leader she can use other people's talents to the full. In addition, there is a great need for learning tolerance since it will be impossible for every member of the group to fulfil exactly what the group expects and, therefore, she will need to learn to understand not only the abilities of others but also their failings and how they can best be helped.

There will also be many occasions when the child will be working alone and in this case it will be necessary for her to know how to organise her own activity, where she will be able to turn for help and what she will be able to do when help is not immediately forthcoming, since obviously the teacher will not be able to deal immediately with every request the child makes for assistance.

It would seem from this that the amount of activity the child undertakes during the course of the day is extensive, and the whole question of homework needs to be re-thought. So far as Vauxhall Manor is concerned there are many children with very few facilities at home for doing their own work and very little parental understanding of the necessity for some time for private study. For this reason the amount of homework that is expected is limited, but there will be times when the child with a rather more understanding and supportive home will be able to continue to study on her own.

Clearly, this way of working is extremely sophisticated. It not only puts great demands upon the child, but it encourages each child to take responsibility and to develop considerable powers of judgement and of reasoning. If this is happening inside the classroom situation and the teacher's role has moved away from the traditional authoritarian one that is usual in the classroom where instruction is provided by the teacher only, then the position of the teacher outside the classroom needs to be re-thought. It is very difficult to change from this kind of senior adviser in the classroom to an authoritarian figure imposing traditional rules outside. We have found at Vauxhall Manor the importance of developing our School Advisory Council and, although we have still a long way to go, we have found the pupils ready to bring this kind of responsibility and thoughtful attitude from their work into a consideration of the whole school organisation. Their tolerance, their understanding and their respect for others have been quite remarkable and their ability to work not only inside their own School Advisory Council group but also in discussion with staff on syllabus and curriculum and standards of work, as well as their ability to make contact with the Parent/Teacher Association and to work with the School Governors, have all indicated the ways in which a school can develop to everyone's benefit from this kind of beginning.

It is important, however, to remember that not all children find this kind of thing easy to do and that all the time teachers have to be aware of the likelihood of children finding this situation well beyond their ability to cope with.

Constant encouragement, a feeling of working together, an understanding of people's weaknesses and a realisation that everyone is there to help everyone else are probably the biggest features of a school like this and certainly there is no doubt that it can be an extremely happy and fruitful place in which to live and to work.

Chapter 4
Sir Leo Schultz High School

A.M. Hunt

The Sir Leo Schultz High School opened in Hull on 6 January 1966, the second of the city's Comprehensives planned under their reorganisation scheme (David Lister High School, headed by the inimitable Albert Rowe, had opened already in September 1964). Unlike David Lister however, Schultz opened with only a few of its purpose-built blocks available and with a roll of 137 pupils and ten staff. Situated in a brand new estate in north Hull, the school grew steadily as the estate opened up and people moved out from the old area off Hessle Road down near the city centre. An impetus to the school's growth was given by the closure of the previous High School for Arts and Crafts on the Head's retirement and the transfer of over 100 pupils and some four or five staff to Schultz (the Authority's well-equipped and well-used Education Centre is now situated in the premises of the previous High School for Arts and Crafts). By September 1966 nearly 750 pupils aged eleven to eighteen had been enrolled at Schultz and this number rose steadily over the next two years, to a peak of 1475 in 1968/1969. From this point on, the Authority's plan for Middle (nine to thirteen) and Senior (thirteen to eighteen) High Schools began to take effect and over the next two to three years numbers in the school settled around the 1100 mark with a staff totalling approximately seventy, including part-timers.

Because of its location, Hull falls naturally into three parts - east of the River Hull (not to be confused with the Humber), west of the same river, and an area to the north of the old city, centred on the University and College of Education and bordering on the "largest village in England" - Cottingham. As much, one imagines, by the grace of God as by the long-term forward planning of the LEA, each of these three "regions" offered a variety of good Junior and Secondary Modern schools readily adjustable for Middle school use, and, in addition, each region had a representative quota of what had been "Selective" schools. The reorganisation scheme envisaged - and effected - the building of at least two "Comprehensive" schools, purpose-built, in each of the regions. Thus starting from scratch in 1964, the Hull LEA put into action and completed its plan in less than a decade, an accomplishment achieved with typical Yorkshire aplomb and without the publicity-seeking accompaniments of so many other LEAs who managed much less in a far greater time span.

Schultz was typical in design of the new purpose-built Comprehensives - thirteen blocks in all, linked by covered ways and encompassing separate accommodation for Technical Studies, Arts and Crafts, Physical Education, Science and General Subjects. A separate Library block was provided as well as a Youth Wing and houses for the resident Chief Caretaker and Maintenance Engineer. At Schultz too a specially built TV Centre housed the LEA's Closed Circuit TV, linked to every school in the city via the local Rediffusion landline. But of all the purpose-built blocks (and it is fair to say that the purpose of some of the blocks, notably the main "Teaching Block", eluded most of us completely during my time there) there is no doubt that the five House blocks were the most "purposeful" of all and were an integral feature of the arrangements we made for our mixed ability work.

I have mentioned already the basic difference between the arrangements for opening Schultz in January 1966 and the starting of David Lister High School in September 1964 - only a handful of pupils were admitted to Schultz initially whilst Lister received almost its full complement more or less overnight. And these differing arrangements made an enormous change in at least one vital area of organisation - the staffing of the school. For whereas David Lister

High School served to "clear" several existing schools (and thus inevitably "received" many of their "redundant" staff), Schultz's only staff additions of this nature came from the High School for Arts and Crafts - less than a handful in a staff which very quickly numbered over fifty.

There is no doubt in my mind that this aspect of the initial organisation was vital at the commencement of our plans for the creation of the sort of flexible arrangements which we considered necessary in a newly opened, developing school feeling its way along new and largely untried lines. The first appointments themselves were absolutely crucial, for they included not only the two Senior Deputies (both now Heads) but also the first House Heads who initially "doubled" as Departmental Heads as well. From the time these posts were advertised, it was made clear that men and women were wanted who could be prepared really to be *Heads* of school houses, acting on an autonomous basis inside a general "brief" and liaising with each other through their own meetings and with their own appointed chairman, rather than through a hierarchical system which laid down all procedures etc. from above to what I call "mini-heads" - much more the norm I have seen even in those Comprehensives progressive enough to have a house system which is truly pastoral and yet at the same time linked to the academic organisation of the place.

Of course, our purpose-built house units helped enormously here - each house reported, assembled, dined, relaxed, *as a house.* House activities were established both in and out of school time and each head of house had his own House/Parents' Association with its own organising committee as well as some form of House Council involving students and staff. As the school developed from 1966 to 1968/1969 an increasing emphasis was placed on the House Head and his role as both academic and pastoral "leader" of a smaller "unit" in the school - thus pupils at Schultz whilst firmly "housed" in a community of less than 300 pupils and twenty staff, where there was a "Head" to whom they were directly accountable, had all the facilities, resources and staff talent of a very large establishment available to them equally - and they knew it.

The LEA's plans for entry to Senior High Schools gave us usually about 320 pupils in our "intake", graded by a system of internal

tests and subjective teacher judgements in the feeder Middle schools
(numbering seven or eight normally) in five grades ("A" - "E") on a
basis supposed to represent a normal curve of distribution. Pupils
and their parents were given a choice of houses they wished to join
- most children merely indicated those friends they wished to be
with - and the school's intake co-ordinator and director of studies
then saw to it that, in general terms, each house "received"
approximately eighty pupils "matched" in the "A" - "E" grades, in
fact a "balanced" quarter of the full intake. The fifth school house,
Schultz House, was developed as a Sixth Form College on the site.
Although each house intake was then divided in the normal way
into three mixed ability tutor groups, within two years of opening
we were abandoning the idea of teaching these groups always simply
as tutor groups. Instead we began sending the whole of the house
"population" in any one year to a school department as a unit -
eighty pupils, at least three, more often four, staff, and a variety of
teaching "areas" available, all leading to much greater flexibility in
our arrangements than had been possible with the "straight" mixed
ability tutor group. Let me make this quite plain, the basis of our
work was mixed ability: this was true from the start and it remained
so when we moved to the house-population idea. Why did we make
this change?

We were working in a new and largely untried area. Whilst we all
wanted to have a flexible and open-minded approach to the problems
of organising the teaching situation in the school, and whilst we were
all firmly of the opinion that we should move away increasingly
from the sacred "class" (streamed and setted) into a more "mixed"
situation, we were very conscious also that we could not over-
experiment with those children already in the school whose time
with us was limited. Our own discussions and the occasional evidence
we could glean from elsewhere led us to the belief that the basic
problem of the "simple" mixed ability class group was that it relied
more than ever on the specific ability of the individual subject
teacher - and this in a teaching situation for which none of us had
been trained and where only a few people had any sort of relevant
experience - except insofar as really gifted teachers tend anyhow to
teach all groups (however arranged) in what I would call a "mixed
ability way", that is, by individualising learning wherever possible.
Instead, we wanted to have a staff "team" available where people
could learn from each other more naturally, where staff "strengths"

could be deployed and "weakness" helped, and where there was a built-in opportunity to re-arrange groups in various ways to suit specific situations.

Of course, therefore, this team-teaching situation in the school could have led to the emergence of groups other than mixed ability - setting, for example, was possible theoretically (although it could only have been over one quarter of the school population in any year). At that stage in the school's development, I believe that this was the right thing to do. Rather than foist mixed ability teaching willy-nilly on uncertain and unready colleagues, I preferrred to build on the mixed ability work which had been going on from the start in most of the Humanities subjects, as well as in Arts, Crafts and Technical Studies. The point is that mixed ability teaching became so much the norm in the school that staff generally were loathe to depart from it, seeing in it so many of the answers to problems of selection inside the school (with the concurrent rejection of some pupils). Thus although Languages notably, and Mathematics and - to a lesser extent - Science, all flirted with more traditional forms of grouping pupils, by 1969/1970 all work in the intake year was based on mixed ability inside the house population.

By this time, we were a 13+ intake school and at the end of a one year's basic course, all pupils were able to opt for two year courses in individual or integrated subjects for the rest of their time in the general school. Again, the timetable was organised on a house population basis, although two houses were inter-related to give greater viability in subject options. Although advice and guidance were given, both from within the school and by visiting Careers Officers, to students and their parents, the final choice was in the hands of the consumers, the pupils themselves. This led inevitably to mixed ability groupings in almost all areas in the senior part of the school, underpinned by continuing mixed ability work in English, Mathematics and Community Studies, the three basic elements still common to everyone's field of study. As the 1970s started, the beginning of mixed ability teaching was moving up into the "new" Sixth Form, "open" already since its inception and where a "tradition" of mixed ability teaching in General Studies had been set up since the opening of Schultz House in 1967.

In a sense then, the conditions for mixed ability teaching at Schultz were created by the way in which the school opened (with an initial intake of 137 mainly ex-Secondary Modern pupils, age eleven to fourteen, rising to about 300 by the end of the first two terms, "mixed" classes were the order of the day from the start); by the chance offered to recruit staff generally with a positive commitment to a school community firmly wedded to the notion of giving all pupils a genuine educational opportunity regardless of "innate ability", IQ and all the other trappings of the previous separatist system; and by the purpose-built nature of the school with its excellent facilities and resources.

The other "conditions" which seem in retrospect to have contributed greatly to the move towards mixed ability work are more difficult and tenuous and thus less easy to describe. They include, though, a much greater involvement in the process of policy making and forward planning for all members of staff, not merely the Head and a small hierarchy, and a cycle of various meetings was used as a means - not always successfully - of allowing everyone to participate as much as he or she wished. Similarly there was a resolve at all levels to "win" parents towards understanding and accepting the school's philosophy and practice, and certainly many of them were more *au fait* with what went on in the school than has been the case in other places where I have worked. Attempts (slowly successful) were made also to involve pupils, especially sixth formers, in real discussions about the school and what it stood for. But a more positive "condition" seems to have been the pattern of staff/student relationships which emerged over the years. Difficult to describe adequately, this was based on the well-established principles of mutual respect, tolerance and understanding, but it went deeper than this, largely, I believe, because almost 100 per cent of our pupils did realise that our total educational concern for them was absolutely and genuinely fundamental to the whole "way of life" in the school. Once an atmosphere of this sort is engendered its effect in a truly educational sense is immense and I believe that it was this sort of "ethos" which, above all, created the conditions we needed to press forward with our mixed ability teaching programmes.

This is not the place for any *detailed* analysis of these programmes but perhaps some brief observations and comments on the application of mixed ability techniques in the more "academic" areas of the curriculum would be appropriate - for, of course, mixed ability work in Art, Craft, Physical Education, etc. have long been the norm.

English and Humanities: A good deal of mixed ability work was initiated from the school's opening, mainly through the use of worksheets, "lead" lessons, visual and aural stimulation, individual project work and so on. The school's Remedial ("Opportunity") Department operated on a withdrawal basis, attempting to "cure" retardation to the point where almost all pupils could be integrated into the school's normal teaching programme with only occasional "reference back" to the remedial area itself. This work, mainly concerned with basic reading and comprehension, was the province of an experienced teacher who had the status - and salary - of other general Heads of Department in the school, and who was assisted wholly by the intake co-ordinator and in part by other members of staff with special interest and skills in remedial work. Quite simply the Opportunity Department attempted to "free" itself of its existing "clients" at the end of the first year of study in the school (i.e. by the 14+ stage). By and large, it succeeded, so that only a handful of pupils with specific and intense learning difficulties were to be found there from the 14+ "options" stage onwards.

Mathematics: Operating along SMP lines, this department moved from "setting" inside the house populations to more genuine mixed ability work, using its own prepared worksheets and setting up its own resources area for individual and remedial work.

Science: Again, internally prepared worksheets were a special feature of the department's programme. More time and thought was given to the setting up of a series of experiments around which students could move rather than to the more normal "demonstration" and follow-up. The scientists set up and developed their own resources area both for individual research for more able students and to give special help and advice to the less able.

Languages: All pupils entering at 13+ took a minimum one year's course in this department. French was taught in all feeder High Schools and the house population of some eighty to ninety students went to the Languages Department at one time. Re-grouping inside this population began to take place at an early stage, "hardening" after Option choices had been made during the Easter term. At this point, some pupils started studying a second foreign language

(German) also; others continued with French; a third group commenced an introductory course in European Studies, which was, for some, the start of a two years' depth course and for others, a final look at possibilities in the languages field - at least for a year or two.

Examination Results: The bare statistics of examination results have been misused so much in recent years by people with various axes to grind that I shall merely limit myself to saying that our results were never disastrously bad, showed a steady improvement, and occasionally were quite outstanding - this was particularly true of English, a Department which, led by a very gifted exponent of mixed ability work, taught in this fashion up to "O" level/CSE. What evidence I accumulated pointed to the fact that, whilst really able students did as well as one could expect under any system, those in the middle range tended to obtain better results than might have been forecast earlier in the school - but, of course, teacher - and pupil - expectations are important in this connection.

The "Open" Sixth Form: Members of the first comprehensive intake reached the sixth form in September 1971 but an "open" sixth form for students transferring from elsewhere as well as for those already in the school (the ex-Secondary Modern pupils who had joined us from 1966 onwards) had been established from 1967. This offered typical "A" level and "O" level courses for candidates who embraced a wider spectrum than usual, and the course in General Studies (which served as a common core for all sixth form students) developed along mixed ability lines from its inception. From 1973 onwards, CSE courses in Creative Arts, Environmental Studies and Humanities began to develop, also along mixed ability lines. Teaching techniques developed in earlier years were adapted and applied at sixth form level - and of course, students were in the sort of teaching/ learning environment to which they had already become used in their time at the school.

Some Further Points:

a) **Books** - textbooks suitable for mixed ability teaching are difficult to find, for few basic texts have been structured to meet the needs of the mixed ability group. Apart from having a wide range of texts and other materials available in a resources centre (surely a necessity for mixed ability work), it is necessary for Departments to draw up their own worksheets. Usually this needs to be done on a team basis with one member of staff acting as leader. The object of the exercise is to introduce into each worksheet a basic core of information so structured that all pupils can comprehend it plus various lines of enquiry/investigation which can be used to the point where every pupil is being "stretched" academically (for the ablest pupils this may mean lines of research beyond the worksheet itself being indicated in it.)

b) **Marking** - marks such as A - E or 0 - 10 can hardly be applied in the traditional sense. Individual assessment is needed with comments rather than marks, matching the pupil against his own best work rather than comparing it with someone else's. Such assessments and comments are probably best made with each pupil personally but this creates great problems of time in the classroom. How far and at what stage are pupils capable of *self*-assessment?

c) **Flexibility** - the move to mixed ability teaching tends to demand a re-think of the traditional timetable and its norms. Often this first shows in a desire for blocks of time to facilitate team-teaching, "lead-in" lessons, films and so on. In this way, a "population" of say ninety pupils across the ability range can meet initially in smaller groupings, then get together for a film or lecture, and then sub-divide in various ways for follow-up activities. Once flexibility of this sort is introduced along with the development of more enquiry-based methods and the extended staff discussions needed for team-teaching work, there is a tendency towards more planned integration across subject divisions either regularly or at least on an occasional basis.

d) **Duration of Unstreaming** - the mixed ability group seems particularly well suited to the lower end of the Secondary School, i.e. for at least the first three years in an all-through eleven to eighteen Comprehensive. Where there is a system of course selection or subject options from the fourth year on, groupings will be more self-determined but may still be largely mixed ability. It is becoming increasingly common for English and Humanities to be retained on a mixed ability basis even to the end of the fifth year.

e) **Implications for Staff** - It is only now that the mixed ability techniques fostered in Comprehensives over the past ten years are (slowly) being introduced into the method courses of some of our

Colleges of Education. Teachers working in mixed ability schools have to accept that their "in-service" training needs will be all the greater for their lack of experience and training in mixed ability work but, against this, there is a natural move in such schools towards the sort of "open doors" policy which enables teachers to "learn on the job" much more quickly than in any traditional situation. In addition, schools running mixed ability courses tend to give much time and energy to organising in-service work on the spot for newcomers, especially probationers - at Schultz a senior member of staff acted as a "James" professional tutor. Most teachers new to mixed ability teaching tend, during the initial stages, to teach to the "middle" of the group, then to group inside the group (to "micro-stream"), and finally to get to the point of considering each member of the teaching group as an individual. Given the right conditions, including the right attitude on the teacher's part (cf. Educational Research News No. 8. January 1970) this usually does not take as long as one might expect.

I have already outlined the basic "conditions" which I feel were vital constituents in our planning for mixed ability work, notably the creation of a real "Comprehensive ethos" in the school, seen most obviously in the quality of the relationships which developed. But, of course, there was more to it than that: we probably started in the only proper way (with small numbers); the calibre of the staff was well above the average; we had almost all of the material, organisational and human facilities that any "Comprehensivist" could want. Our more academically inclined pupils could get all that they would have got in a traditional Grammar School, plus a real sense of community with the diversity of less academically inclined pupils with whom they had always shared classes. A great deal of incidental - but nevertheless vital - learning went on in the wide range of "mixed ability" clubs and societies which abounded, catering for individual interests and talents. The school's educational guidance services operated a continuous programme which helped each individual to channel himself or herself in accordance with abilities, interests, job prospects, and so on. School reports were made in an honest and positive way and were soon readily accepted by employers as complementary to a pupil's examination results. Examinations themselves were approached in a no fuss, no nonsense, no "life or death" spirit. The whole emphasis was on learning largely through pupil activity with teacher guidance, using TV and audio-visual aids, programmed learning, team teaching and so on as very important but subsidiary devices to the teaching and learning principles embodied in the very structure and atmosphere of the school. Given such conditions, backed by a helpful and non-interferring local authority, mixed ability work could - and did - thrive. Not being an out and out idealist, I will not go on to claim that, given such conditions, it can right almost all of the wrongs which beset contemporary society. Instead I will content myself merely with the practical conclusion that, in the right circumstances, mixed ability teaching has a great deal to offer academically as well as socially to all our pupils.

Chapter 5
Milefield Middle School

T. Gannon, O.B.E.

The Middle school is a comparative newcomer to the educational
scene in Great Britain. This is true, I must hasten to add, only of the
state maintained system in England and Wales, since Scotland keeps
its children at Primary school until the age of twelve and the Private
or Preparatory day or boarding school has always catered for the
eight to thirteens as a separate discrete group, preparing them by the
Common Entrance examination for selective secondary education.
The term "Middle school" as applied to this age-range, housed in a
separate building, under an independent and separate administration,
implies however, for the state sector, an entirely novel institution. It
is different both in concept and philosophy from the Scottish or
private pattern and similar to them solely, and in part only, in the
age groups it embraces. This case study covers the five year infancy
of one of the first state Middle schools, the first in fact to be custom-
built for children of the specific age-range nine to thirteen. It will
thus be different both in character and content from the other four
under review since it will concern itself *ipso facto* with previously
untried groupings of children over the age of eleven with others
below that age, brought together in a novel context and setting.
Young as this one school and its contemporaries are, many local

education authorities began very quickly to introduce similar schools into their plans for secondary re-organisation, so that three tier systems of First, Middle, and High schools are already well established, both in numbers and geographical spread as the latest pattern of comprehensive education.

It was noted by Fred Clarke at the beginning of the Second World War that the underlying reasons for division into different types of school were *"much less educational than they ought to be"*; they were more likely to be *"social, administrative and historical"*.[1] No doubt this new kind of tripartism too was fashioned like its predecessor out of pragmatism and expediency, but it came at a time when sound educational reasons were being advanced for a fresh look at the whole spectrum of child education, school and pre-school, and, even where expediency has played a major part in the acceptance or rejection of three-tier systems, the very breadth and sweep of the changes involved have created a climate for re-appraisal and particularly so for the middle years of schooling. The Plowden report, then newly minted, had expressed unease about the large numbers in many Secondary schools and the lengthy span of a possible seven years in such schools. Girls entered in the pre-pubertal stage and left as nubile, soon to be franchised young women; boys came at the receiving end like Shakespeare's schoolboy *"with shining morning face"* and left, sometimes literally, as *"soldiers bearded like the pard"*.

To doubts about the wisdom of associating these dissimilar, widely separated age groups under one roof and under the umbrella of a common, subject based, examination-orientated curriculum were added fears that the younger fry, the eleven to thirteens, suffered too early and too great a "sea change" from their primary days in a social sense too.

The danger was ever present that some of their prime needs could be lost sight of in the massive presence of the Secondary school, its size, numbers and weight of older sophisticated students whose identity was with peer groups only. These and other reservations were summed up by Plowden[2] in the succinct assertion that *"The experience of teachers and many other educationalists suggests that for many children the changes of curriculum and method associated with a break at eleven cut across a phase in learning and in attitudes to it"*.

It would be quite wrong to infer from this that Secondary schools, large or small are unaware of the needs and particular attributes of children in these middle years of schooling. Many indeed arrange highly sophisticated and carefully planned semi-independent systems of organisation within the total school complex to ensure that this group is catered for with a prior regard for their needs as they are seen to be *at that stage of their lives.* Many go much further to carry out the dictum of an American educationalist that *"Middle school children need something that will be theirs and theirs alone."*[3] Middle schools after all will cater in the foreseeable future for only one quarter of the age groups concerned and it would be foolish to assert that such schools by their very existence alone will make a necessarily better showing than those catering for the other three quarters. If it is accepted, however that eleven is too tender an age to break off from *"the best practices of the Primary school"*, a plea must be entered that wherever the eleven to thirteens find them-selves, in Middle schools, or with the majority, they be treated as part of the span from eight to thirteen.

Just as there is a danger of taking too jaundiced a view of some Secondary school practice and provision, an over-effusive admiration for all things primary has its perils and illusions. There is a tendency to idealise the teacher of juniors as one, in the poet's words, *"who walks in beauty like the night";* the maternal or paternal central figure who sees the child's learning process as a whole, who considers and uses the child's environment for experience based learning, who matches the work and its pace to the individual child. Impeccable sentiments these, and the Middle school, any school, for any age, does need the traditional Primary school strength of security and personal relationships of good quality between teacher and taught. Important too for all successor schools to emulate is the wise way of the good Primary teacher who, whilst keeping an eye on the stages reached by his individual charges in various aspects of learning and the curriculum, pays even greater attention to the individual's *work rate* and constantly asks himself of the work "Why is it getting better, or worse, or remaining static?"

These are matters of approach and attitude. It is when consideration of curricular practices and the resources to carry them out come into the account that some real concern is felt and shown, not least of course, and in fact mostly by Primary teachers themselves. Most irritating for them, since the responsibility for its continuance and power to redress it lies beyond their control, is the lack of staffing and other resources to provide other than a restricted curricular diet. Older Primary school children in particular can suffer from inadequate provision. In certain specific curricular fields such as Modern Languages, Science, Music and possibly Mathematics, inadequate staffing and technical resources, at a time when they are most, not least, needed, store up problems for the future as well as creating them for the immediate present. The consequent inhibition of studies to the depth of which their teachers know such children are capable is a continuous source of anxiety. A secondary danger, of which again experienced Primary teachers are well aware, also follows from the deficiencies mentioned.

Attempts to counteract the deficiencies or minimise their effect by means of superficial overall themes or topics which supposedly "integrate" the curriculum can end in shallow performance levels and confusion of aims and purposes by both teachers and taught. This is in no way to denigrate the many excellent themes or projects undertaken by Junior schools, from which we learn so much. In every case, these are most successful when the teacher partners cut the coat according to the cloth, in other words limit the experience to the bounds of the possible. A salutary reminder of the confusion created by over-enthusiasm lies in the answer of the eleven year old who was asked *"Why do you think we are doing these subjects together?"*, and replied *"Because we are not clever enough to do them separately."*

Sometimes too, enthusiasm for the maternal or paternal role can be carried too far, and over-protectiveness from the primary approach can stifle the curiosity and readiness to "have a go" of the Junior school child. Too much shelter, it may be said, can keep out the sun as readily as the driving rain. One reasonable argument for the setting up of Middle schools must surely be that they will be in a better posture from a staffing and resources viewpoint to continue with less frustrations than the Primary schools, the *"best Primary practices"* so sought after by them both. They will have, certainly they ought to have, even in the least favoured areas, a staffing establishment that will permit the enlistment of specialist subject teachers alongside experienced Primary staff. They will find places for those trained by former combined Junior/Secondary courses in addition to the

intake from the ever increasing numbers of those trained specifically
for Middle schools. This combination of type and quality of teaching
resources in such a rich and variegated mixture is unlikely to be
found in any other kind of school, not even in the largest and best
equipped of the Primaries. It follows that a firm base is almost
assured for the setting up of a variety of mixed ability groupings
since a large proportion of the staff will be familiar with or have
received training in approaches based on such groupings, while
others who have some special skill or expertise to offer, but have
never deployed their talents in such fashion, will have experienced
colleagues to *"guide them"* in the words of the Psalmist, *"along the
right path"*.

Before going on to consider the working pattern of one such school,
it seems pertinent to point out that although teaching and learning
via mixed ability groups and individual group assignments seems the
logical approach to adopt, there will be a need, given the ever-
widening gap in extent and range of individual abilities and aptitudes
as children pass through these explosive middle years, to make some
provision for work outside the class groupings. This need will be seen
to occur particularly for the groupings in Modern Languages and
Mathematics in so far as slow-learning children are concerned on the
one hand, and for the most able in such subjects on the other.

There follows the implication from this with which Middle school
teachers concur, that the teachers too are a mixed ability bunch on
any staff, differing not simply in the sense of having a mixture of
capabilities in differing specialist fields, but mixed in terms of the
ability to display their own or cope with children's skills under
differing group arrangements. Wise teachers will accept that this is so,
since it in no way diminishes their status but rather enhances it. As
one learns to admire the skills and arts of other craftsmen or profes-
sionals in other occupations by simple straightforward observation,
or even more profoundly by some understanding of what is entailed
in their performance, so teachers should be admired and recognised
for qualities observed or particular facets of skill displayed and
particularly so by their colleagues who see these at close quarters.

The discernment that comes from working closely with other
teachers and the ability to profit from the relationships involved are
arrived at only by the use of certain skills and attitudes by all

concerned. The ability to assess, to evaluate, to co-ordinate the work of all the group might require perhaps a higher order talent and outlook which possibly only experience would bring in its train. The skill of one teacher in stimulating and holding the interest of large groups of children and the artistry required to do this is balanced by that of another who shows herself as a skilful practitioner with small groups; the teacher who is receptive to new ideas and quick to grasp and develop their potential usefulness has a counterpart who initiates new ideas or ways of tackling a theme or topic perhaps, and in persuasive discussion with his colleagues plots the probable course and outcome of their adoption by the group.

Few teachers would claim to be able to look at the world of the child as a whole, or to be able to meet as an individual even the most straightforward and simple basic needs, however differently these would be considered by individual teachers.

Teachers working singly all the time and over a long period, perhaps inevitably and unconsciously are prone to take on the mantle of the child critic rather too readily. Their entirely laudable anxiety to fulfil the child's interests and ensure his progress, when they are almost the sole arbiters of this progress and uniquely responsible for it, inclines them to a demanding rather than an accepting relationship with their classes which is difficult to stifle or subdue. Even less happily on occasions, critical judgement is passed on the performance of colleagues and particularly of the teacher who has had the longest immediate spell of previous responsibility for the class they teach now. A teacher who grumbled in this fashion after a short sojourn with his new class with the remark, *"This class knows damn all"*, received some useful advice and a deserved rebuke from a colleague with the rejoinder, *"If they can spell it, start from there!"* The two great difficulties facing teachers about applying any kind of pressure on children are knowing when to start the application, and, more importantly, when to stop it.

The child's need for love and security, for praise and recognition, for new kinds of experience, for success in some such new experience, and, however ill-equipped he or she seems for it, the need to be given some measure of responsibility for something or someone would rank high in priority for most teachers. One could enlarge and go on adding to this list in terms of individual children in a particular school or locality, but enough skills have been enumerated to indicate the need to pool the strengths of the staff so that, as teachers become more sensitive and attuned to each other and thus more sensitive to children, they can build on the wish to succeed and harness the often well-concealed yearning of even those least likely to achieve success.

We are none of us unaware of the educational perils summed up in the homely adage *"More haste less speed"*. We ourselves tend to overlook the rapidity of the pace of events, the newness of the world, the imminence of social change. We may assume unthinkingly the child's ability to absorb and adjust to the helter-skelter world about him rather than to marvel at the self-defensive internal mechanism with which in fact he does adjust to the bewildering abnormalities of "normal" daily life. Consider the true tale of the eleven year old girl who was asked *"Where did you go for your holidays this year?"* and answered *"Majorca, Miss"*. When then posed the good teacher's follow-up question, *"Where is that?"*, she replied - *"Don't know, Miss. We flew."* There can be other hasty or ill-digested experiences of a similar kind in the classroom, perhaps stemming from an attempt to catch up with a deadline set by a syllabus or an examination.

We now turn to a survey of the particular Middle school, "Milefield", whose working philosophy has to some extent already been revealed. It has tried to follow, over a period of six years, with staff, pupils and often also extraneous but extremely co-operative educational institutions and individuals, a working pattern based on mixed ability groups with concern for the individuals within such groups. Milefield is one of thirteen Middle schools of the nine to thirteen variety, all pioneer schools of this type, which opened simultaneously in the West Riding six years ago.[4] It serves, from Grimethorpe, the three contiguous villages of Brierley, Grimethorpe and Shafton which are mainly coal-mining communities with peripheral mixed farming. Three First Schools for the five to nines send their children to Milefield, and, as one of three Middle schools together covering a wider-based group of villages, Mielfield in turn feeds a Senior High school for the thirteen to eighteens, also based in the largest village, Grimethorpe. There thus emerges a "pyramid pattern" of schools of all. the three types with the Senior High school at the apex, three contributory Middle schools below and nine First schools at the base. Unusually, one imagines, for such a small place as Grimethorpe, one may go from "unifix to university entrance" without, in some cases, a walk of more than ten minutes between schools.

With minimal movement of pupils or their families outside this structure, the opportunities for contact, laterally and vertically, are thus significantly greater than would be possible for large and complex urban areas, whose populations engage in a variety of major and minor industries. Here "King Coal" reigns supreme, a vital and once again a growth industry, and there is the close-knit family sense, based on common purpose and experience, of the mining communities. The concern of the generality of mining families for their children's education is a known phenomenon, as is their readiness to participate in and support any action that will further their children's education interest and welfare at school. No doubt because of the close sense of reliance upon each other bred by the uncongenial work and its dangers, they understand very clearly the implications of the Plowden Report's plea to parents that their concern and responsibilities should be "joint as well as several".

In "Teaching Mixed Ability Classes", the problems, more the perils of essaying team teaching or other forms of grouping where the teachers are not reasonably within range of each other and their pupils for consultation and discussion have been clearly signposted.[5] Milefield is purpose-built, and perhaps there is no escaping the fact that the roles of teachers in such schools, like those of their colleagues in adapted premises, may be crucially determined and partially conditioned by the accommodation and facilities available. No limits however can be set on the ingenuity and resourcefulness of any individual staff other than those which they themselves determine, and in this sense no two schools even purpose-built to the same identical pattern should or need too closely resemble each other, apart from the style of building. The parent book also warns of the folly of the *"play it by ear and see what happens"* approach founded on a confused and distorted definition of freedom. This is a salutary warning for the purpose-built or any other kind of Middle school where it would certainly not be politic to emulate Graves' cabbage-white butterfly and *"fly from here to there by guess by God by hope and hopelessness"*. Conversely, all such schools are to some degree only freshly emerged from the chrysalis, and it would be equally impolitic to become definitive about the task of the teachers in these early years of establishment. There is the danger that like the Prince in Hamlet the new schools will become *"the glass of fashion and the mould of form"*, following an inevitable period as the *"observed of all observers"*, and take a form of blue-print teaching design to match the architect's drawing. The tendency to talk about "open-plan teaching" is already a source of distress to those teachers who rightly regard such terms as a simplification for a much more demanding and complex teaching skill.

In any school, and, to a correspondingly greater degree, in a school both new and purpose-built with a novel age-group, tensions will arise - necessary tensions which inspire needed changes in practice and direction if fruitfully resolved, discomfort and diminished responses from staff if not thrashed out or left unresolved. In the chapter on team-teaching, a number of salient points are made in the parent book about the collaboration of staff for this purpose and particularly that such co-operation is but *"one aspect of a wider collaboration within the school"*. At the outset, this wished for creation of a wider and deeper relationship was expressed at Milefield through the mundane and much abused idea of partnership between children, teachers and parents. The term "parent" had a broader reference to include all other responsible relatives of the children and indeed any persons disposed to show interest in the school's welfare or that of those few children in particular whose links with adults other than their teachers were sometimes tenuous and strained, and regrettably interrupted on occasions by dissension and, more rarely, violence.

Partners too were considered all who had professional links with the school in the administrative sense and, very particularly so, the internal, domestic, school meals and ancillary staff. For the teacher-child working relationship there seemed to be an analogy with the call used in country dancing "Partners in the Middle". There is required from the dancers when this call is made, orally or by a musical signal, a well-defined variation of movement and change of pace and steps. The dancers leave their original bases make new formations with different partners, rejoin their initial partners and return to base again. Re-assuring the hesitant and the novice an experienced partner aided by the rhythmic beat of the music puts out a firm, decisive guiding arm. The parallel for school seems fairly exact, the same secure base is needed, the dependable rhythm, the controlled coming and going, the change and exchange of partners at the appropriate time and place.

At Milefield I sought before we opened, with the aid of the senior experienced staff who had opted for posts at the school, a pattern of organisation which would allow flexibility in the roles of the staff, so that questions of conciliation and reconciliation as between partners, were brought more directly within the teacher's province.

There was not only to be delegated responsibility where appropriate but executive authority to carry out ideas and decisions arrived at by joint planning with minimum referral beyond the group concerned, except for, rarely it was hoped, last-ditch arbitration in an unresolved dispute. Such a sharing of functions, it was thought, would influence the staff to consider their relationship with children to be such that on occasions they, the teachers, would accept the novel role of learners with and from children and other colleagues. There would be a two-way traffic of ideas between teachers and taught with the emphasis on production rather than reproduction, expression rather than impression, in all the activities they undertook. If children were to be accepted as partners and they themselves accept and understand the implications of this, the building of a secure base was vital. We hoped that one corner-stone would be the known rapport between teacher and parent established on a basis of mutual understanding and frankness (no pulling of punches), wherever and as quickly as it could be laid in place. Another would be the organisation itself, freed from public examinations or external curricular pressure, preferring co-operation to competition as befitting partners, aiming to promote personal growth and to induce children to become creative in a variety of different ways. Given the right choice and supply of materials, opportunities to exploit the skills which would come from confident use of them, and given, above all, wise guidance from teachers willing to share their expertise with their colleagues, the creative urges of the children would, we assumed, to use a cricketing expression, "come good", in the kind of building we had been fortunate enough to inherit.

There was no corresponding feeling among us, the initial staff, of being "purpose-built" for the task, rather a sense of apprehension and an inkling of what the apostle Paul was driving at in expostulating to the Corinthians *"teach ye and advise ye one another in*

wisdom". There were nine men, nine women, seven of whom were
ex-secondary specialists, and eight probationary teachers for whom
this was their first post. Two, only, excluding myself, had any
Primary school experience, and, for all but these three, teaching in
the form of mixed ability groups or by individual assignment was, at
that stage, either a point for discussion in a lecture or something
outside their previous practice as teachers. Since as one of the first
Middle schools, we had no precedents, we were compelled to begin a
dialogue designed for our mutual aid, taking frank account of our
potential strengths and weaknesses, and ranging over all matters
which affected our aims and policies. We considered first the effect
that a modification of the traditional "leadership" role to one of
"partnership" would have on ourselves with our varied backgrounds
and experience, and, in conjunction with that, the children's possible
reactions, given their dissimilar schools, homes and circumstances.
To counter the obvious weakness arising from lack of practice within
the group as an entity, there was the length and breadth of specialist
skills to be drawn upon and the heartening knowledge that the staff's
expertise as a whole covered a very wide curricular field. There were
added bonuses in the shape of enthusiasms which had not formed
part of a traditional college or university course but in which a high
degree of proficiency had been reached through personal practice
and study. Especially, and thankfully, was this so for music, instru-
mental and choral, but such individual delights as mountaineering
and entomology, judo and calligraphy were soon to emerge as added
interests for children's participation and pleasure. A source of most
comfort and strength was the realisation that the group of staff had
opted to meet this challenge and this committal to a joint enterprise
was itself an expression of group identity.

We agreed as a priority that to gain security for each child in this
four-form entry school with four classes of thirty or so children in
each year group, four teachers would each assume responsibility for
a class for their whole stay in any year group for at least one year.
Sixteen teachers were thus committed to the role of class teacher for
the greater part of their time, each having a class base or teaching
space which was theirs.

Thirty children, conversely, always had a teacher who "belonged" to
them. Each of the four classes in the year group had immediate
access by wall-length sliding doors to a year group shared area. There

were further areas for Science, Home Economics, Art and Craft, each specifically equipped for the purpose but less sophisticatedly or elaborately so than in a large Secondary school, and not enclosed, as is the general pattern for secondary provision. There were two halls for P.E., Music and Drama, the larger one reserved in the main for the educational gymnastics type of activity, with the requisite apparatus, the smaller for assemblies, school dinners, class drama, club functions, the usual multi-purpose scope of activities of such nature. A central library and display area facing this smaller open-ended hall, some music practice rooms leading off it and a "quiet room" adjoining the staff-room complete the teaching space provision.

The issue is raised in the companion book's chapter on team-teaching[6] of the delicate balance between decision-making and leadership when any form of group or co-operative effort by staff requires agreed acceptance by all the members involved, and the idea of a rotating chairman for short-term responsibility in turn is favoured. This seems an ideal to aim at, particularly in terms of the more complex executive structure required for older students. For our purposes, where a year group of four staff was the vital core of the team-teaching unit and other teachers were introduced in a variety of patterns for different areas of work, the need for these younger children of an accepted reasonably permanent teacher in charge of proceedings both for teachers and taught seemed paramount. Moreover such a teacher was to be additionally responsible for the pastoral and welfare care of the whole group, the maintenance of the recording systems, the negotiating role with the other three year groups for the deployment of "advisory" teachers and the parent-teacher relationship for the year group. In fact, if not in degree, all the duties normally attributable to the Head except ultimate responsibility and school administration came within the purview of the teacher whose naming as "Head of Year Group" implied the wide-embracing scope of the function. Since this teacher also had a particular responsbility for his or her own class and the class, as stated, was to enjoy its own considerable degree of autonomy, the danger of a "mightier than thou" pose from the Year Group Head was averted. In fact the acceptance of the role and its implications brought from the holders this acute realisation of the need to maintain and preserve democratic procedures and to abjure ideas of maternalism or paternalism, however benevolently intended. A further safeguard against a Year Group Leader acting on the assumption that within his own domain *"L'etat c'est moi"*, was the presence of the three "advisory" teachers mentioned. They met on equally responsible footing with the Year Group Heads, to ensure that they were properly and equitably deployed within the school or within their own specialist areas. The necessarily frequent meetings of the seven that did take place brought keen discussion and hard bargaining for the allocation of the advisers to year groups in turn and in fair proportion and this is a continuing feature to date.

These three senior teachers offered as main interests, and as a matter of curricular policy, specialisms in creative and expressive arts related to the specially equipped areas in the school. They had a definite charge to spread enthusiasm for and knowledge of their own specialisms throughout the school, to act as advisers to staff and children with particular reference to these special fields but none-the-less to give active support, encouragement and sympathy to all the enterprises that their class and year based colleagues undertook. They did this directly on occasions in a classroom, with the class teacher present or not, or with individuals or pairs or small groups as the situation required in their own equipped areas. Indirectly they advised the year group staff on the content and development of year group themes and class topics, and played full supporting roles in the presentation, appreciation, and recording and evaluation of work done by children.

Whatever the specialities of the staff, experienced or otherwise, we felt that the curriculum for this age group should cover five broad complementary areas of "bands" of experience which were defined in subject terms rather than in the "areas of knowledge" divisions adopted by some curricular theorists.[7] This decision was based on the need to assure the secondary specialists on the staff that they had something very valuable to offer in terms with which they were familiar. It was felt too, that the controversy, if such exists, between a "subject" and an "area of knowledge" approach is artificial, since if learning is to take place, or the "learning how to learn" in Bruner's phrase, some bringing together of subject knowledge and a definition of it is required as base or starting point. In the same way teachers recognise that enquiry-based learning involving research is unlikely to happen without good reading proficiency and groupings to acquire or advance this skill are to be given priority at times for some children.

The curriculum then, in subject terms, embraced the following five related areas: Maths/Science, English/R.E., P.E./Music, Modern Language/Social and Environmental Studies and Art/Craft/Home Studies. Setting aside the last of these groups where, as already said, there was considerable advisory specialist skill to hand, the aim from the year group angle was to ensure that for each of the first named elements in each band i.e. Maths, English, P.E., Modern Language (in our case — French), there was a teacher member of the group with a corresponding expertise or interest. Thus for the first two year groups, where almost all the eight staff were able to cope readily with three out of four of these linear sequential activities, and some all four of them, in their mixed ability classes, the interchange of staff beyond the year group for these purposes was kept to an irreducible minimum, and freedom to operate a flexible time table allowing large block periods for work outside the four basic elements was assured.

The main difficulty, as expected, was the fitting in of regular periods of French, not only because every year group's teaching assets in this element were insufficient to cover and give continuity and the necessary regularity for all the year group, but also because of the "sore thumb" syndrome that Modern Language teaching tends to involve. A highly structured course was required to give non-specialist class teachers in the subject support and confidence and to ensure continuity, whilst this clashed with the wish to avoid fragmentation into subject divisions and to permit long uninterrupted periods for theme or topic work. This problem was gradually met by intensive in-service training sessions to help make groups self-supporting, by importing for one or two classes a member of staff from the upper age group in exchange for remedial work by the First Year Head, and by the use of advisory staff who had the ability as a second or even third string to their specialist bows, to teach French at that level. The advisers were also able, during the morning sessions when the basic elements part of the programme were generally conducted, to withdraw small groups for work in the Home Studies space or the workshop, Science or Music areas, or allow one of the resident year group staff to use these resources with children whilst they took over the class role as stated.

For the two upper age-groups the same degree of flexibility, though sought for, was not achieved, since the problems involved in teaching

French and now also Mathematics to entirely mixed groups proved too obdurate. In these two subjects there arose, as time went on, a very wide gap between the least and the most able and the non-specialist class teachers felt themselves unable to meet the differing demands of sub-groups within their classes,especially in French. They were particularly diffident about their capacity to meet the needs of the most able, *under any form of grouping.* Indeed the specialist teachers of French themselves found the process of catering for sub-groups within the class both exhausting and unproductive for childrens' learning. With Mathematics the problem centred round the non-specialist teacher's ability not only to cope with those few individuals whose skills were beginning to surpass the teacher's, but to diagnose the learning difficulties of many who needed skilled attention to the same or greater degree indeed than the few first mentioned.

So as to achieve at least as much possible provision of large blocks of time, if not on the same scale as for the younger children, some breakdown of the class-group into a year group arrangement had to be accepted and thus some essential time-tabling and "setting" for French and Mathematics. Mathematics was much the lesser problem in that the approach was mainly by individual assignment and thus the specialist teachers could, provided that half the year group at a time was engaged in the subject simultaneously, oversee the whole field, giving the required assistance to individual children and their colleagues. The children, therefore, were setted for French, the device being adopted of naming the four groups after the names of large French towns or cities, one group, the most able linguistically, one the least, with two parallel average groups which the non-specialist class teachers felt competent to manage and provide for. With once again half of the year group simultaneously involved, the specialists were able to exert overall supervision and assist colleagues, whilst themselves catering for the least and most able. Once these four French groups were established, there was no necessity, apart from that resulting from close observation of individuals' performances, to regroup them for either P.E. or Mathematics and children returned to their own class teacher for English and related studies to be undertaken at times most convenient for that teacher.

There remained, and again, mainly in the afternoon sessions, long periods of time for class themes or topics and, when advisory staff were allocated, opportunities for mixed ability groups drawn from the whole year to undertake more ambitious studies of selected environmental areas. A year group staff, for example, supplemented by two or three advisers and with the assistance of staff and students of a College of Education, studied the environment and history of a college which had magnificent grounds and a stately home to offer for exploration by staff and children. Such a venture, its organisation and planning are described elsewhere in this book,[8] others on a more limited scale of time and resources involved close studies of the more immediate environment, others yet were so entitled and planned that work in particular disciplines emerged prominently, whilst still encouraging related work in other aspects of the curriculum to be presented, discussed and displayed.

In all this thematic work there would obviously be a prominent featuring of Art and Craft and Home Studies, the last group in our five band curriculum, and also extensive opportunities for the second set of elements in our first four bands, viz., Science, Social and Environmental studies, R.E. and Music, all on a mixed ability group or individual assignment basis and where possible by choice of staff and children conjointly.

It was indicated earlier that a Middle school should concern itself with children as they are seen to be at that stage of their lives and should look closely to the interest and friendship groupings which will promote social confidence as well as curricular skills. This concern should take precedence over the presumed needs of the following stages of their education. Autonomy however is not a synonym of licence, and it is not inconsistent to aver that in the latter years of Middle school life groups and individuals should undertake work that will have a significant repercussion on their entry to further education, because of its more specialised nature and because the teachers in charge of such groups will be, naturally, forceful advocates in the promotion of their particular discipline. One way to do this was to amalgamate sets of twenty, and offer *via* twelve teachers, i.e. the resident eight and four others, the special skills of each of these staff in cyclical pattern at the choice, as far as was possible, of the children in the sets which were of mixed sex, age and ability. They were thus introduced to more intensive courses ranging over three kinds of Science study, Modern Maths, the Visual Arts, Music, Literature, Rural and Social Studies, Movement and

Drama. We hoped that the children would, in the process of sampling these in turn, not only acquire some very desirable chosen skills, but also make shrewd assessments of their own capabilities, make further choices for individual, group or club studies, and feel no lack of confidence when they met up with these interests again in the guise of subjects to be studied at the High school.

Finally, this open-ended arrangement over a block period of time brought other benefits in its train. It permitted some external specialist help to be made available, e.g., the authority's own advisory staff, the staff of the High school, staffs of linked Colleges of Education, parents and other members of the community who because of the time allocation could fit in their contribution at periods most suitable to themselves.

These, then, are some of the ways in which a Middle school in a particular locality gives scope for teachers to play a variety of roles and achieve satisfaction for themselves and their charges. There will be many other and better ways now in operation or being sought for and discussed. In my reckoning, organisation and methods and curriculum content are not in the event the chief factors in determining the quality of schooling in the middle years. They can only follow in the train of an established attitude and relationship based on an understanding of the needs of all the groups and individuals in a certain school, in a certain place, with its own individual staff and very special children. If this is given priority and care taken to ensure good quality of lateral, vertical and tangential communications with all the "partners" involved, the task of providing the right curricular and social background becomes correspondingly less formidable.

The story is told that, when Michelangelo went to see the Pope who was about to engage him to build the dome of St Peter's and paint the Sistine Chapel, he brought with him the following testimonial, *"The bearer of these presents is Michelangelo, the sculptor. His nature is such that he needs to be drawn out by kindness and encouragement, but if love be shown him and he be treated really well he could accomplish things that will make the whole world wonder."*

References

1 Clarke, F., Education and Social Change (1940).
2 Children and their Primary Schools (HMSO 1967), p.142, para. 371.
3 Murphy, J., The American Middle School (1966), p.18.
4. See DES pamphlet, Launching the Middle School (HMSO 1970).
5 Kelly, A.V., Teaching Mixed Ability Classes (Harper & Row 1974), p.35.
6 Kelly, A.V., op. cit., p.37.
7 See, for example, Tyler, R.W., Basic Principles of Curriculum and Instruction (U. of Chicago 1947), Kerr, J.F., Changing the Curriculum (ULP 1968) and Wheeler, D.K., Curriculum Process (ULP 1967).
8 See Chapter 7

Part II
The Teachers and the Subjects

Chapter 6
Art and Craft in the Middle School

B.G. Walker

"The artist discovers in the world around, that is, in his raw materials, relationships, order, harmony, - just as the musician finds these things in the world of sound. This cannot be done by the conscious, scheming, planning mind. Art is not an effort of will but is a gift of grace - to the child at least, the simplest and most natural thing in the world. Whenever people are sincere and free, art can spring up . . . That is why the child's happiness or otherwise in the presence of the teacher is all important, and why the school of today is, or should be, the perfect setting for children's art".

Marion Richardson

This profound statement echoes some of the thoughts and aspirations which were developing in my mind during the 1960s when I was a subject specialist teaching in a Secondary school. As experience grew, I became increasingly uncertain of the motives behind the work I was doing in the Art room - a phase that most teachers go through at some time or another, especially those who think in more creative terms. Inside, I was striving to discover some acceptable formula whereby teacher-motivated work might be replaced by honest and fearless Art, that which communicates the children's own ideas - a true reflection of themselves as people. The production of twenty or thirty pictures emitting virtually the same idea was not the goal I was aiming for.

Art cannot exist in a vacuum, or be engineered at set times of the day or week. Initial concepts ferment, are stirred around in the mind and finally evolve as personal statements. Art is an integral part of life; some would say a vital part. It goes far deeper than study. By its very nature, it passes beyond reasoning to the point where words of explanation become inadequate. Learning is often knowing without feeling. Art is doing what one knows with one's heart in it.

The Secondary school system, as it was then, seemed to place its emphasis on how the subject affected the child rather than upon what the child could make of the subject. In retrospect, I was undoubtedly caught up in this net. With the advent of the Comprehensive system and with fresh thinking about education on all fronts, I suspect that the situation has changed somewhat over the past five years, but without first hand knowledge it would be unwise for me to comment. My own circumstances would be more to the point.

I changed to the Middle school in 1968 with considerable expectation that certain anxieties would be resolved and that the change in education would open up vast possibilities. I was encouraged by the fact that my role as a specialist would show significant changes from that of the teacher in the Secondary school. I would be working alongside other members of staff - an approach hitherto unencountered. The Primary school structural foundation meant that each class teacher would be initially responsible for the art within his (I use the word neutrally) own classroom and that each class would possess its own basic art kit. I would be in a position to help, advise and guide the work indirectly or directly whatever situation occurred and, in like manner, other teachers would claim expertise in academic subjects, special methods of teaching, greater experience in dealing with social needs or in the organisation of classroom activities. All would learn from each other. It would not simply be a case of teachers concentrating on the disciplines of subjects or being involved in the continuation of good Primary class teaching, but a challenging case for what might be termed "mixed ability teachers". The satisfaction of both needs would be achieved by an organisation that would extend beyond the traditional allocation of one teacher to one class.

Within this pattern of approach, a much greater interpretation of child Art was visualised. Much has been discussed about the breaking down of subject barriers and integrating various aspects of learning. In the Middle school, the younger age groups do not require the compartmentalised knowledge embodied in a syllabus based upon the refinements of each subject. On the other hand, the older children need that step forward from concrete operations to a more careful ordering of their knowledge. Perhaps the integration of Art and Craft is much more possible than that of its linear counterparts. I wished to see such integration taking place, but foresaw a danger that complete and total absorption might stifle or obliterate the identity of exciting visual expression. My main consideration, therefore, was not merely to link Art with the rest of school work, but to ensure that by constant reflection and advice there existed a freedom whereby children of all temperaments and backgrounds would be able to present their acquired knowledge in the most natural and expressive way possible. The subsequent advice, the endless discussion, the gentle persuasion and the help I offered to those teachers who displayed initial fears about entering the doors of a mysterious Art world, played a major part in forming acceptable attitudes to what has now evolved as a formidable aspect of the Middle school curriculum.

The approach to the curriculum enabled grouping on the basis of interest rather than ability to take place. The flexibility of the time-table allowed for unbroken opportunities where children could pursue their learning through deepening interests. The purpose-built Middle school enabled children to extend their ideas from the classroom into more specialised areas where new and problematic materials existed.

The ensuing work, crystallising in the classroom, manifesting itself in exciting display, to which everyone contributed, was as refreshingly individualist as it was deeply significant.

Raymond and Clifford, aged twelve, became very interested in the growth and development of some locusts kept in the school's incubator. Their class teacher, a natural scientist, encouraged their involvement in a serious study of the insects. After initial research, the two boys made a reasonably accurate model of a locust from such varied materials as balsa wood, butter muslin, wire, cork and pins. This they showed to me with some pride and satisfaction. As a result of their approach to me I was able to extend their idea into a new medium. They were instructed in the art of brazing and without further encouragement constructed a welded metal sculpture which not only simulated the delicate structure of the insect, but possessed all the exciting qualities of experiment in the boys' new found material. They incorporated a tin can, bottle tops, wire mesh and mild steel rod into their construction, solving all the problems themselves as they progressed. It only remained for me to keep a watchful, yet distant, eye on their labours. The initial spark of interest had come directly from them to their class teacher.

The potentiality of children to create fine things has been grossly underestimated in the past. Children can produce unique works if presented with the opportunity. So much "Art" in school tends to be an activity of "re-creation" which can only be considered irrelevant. The two boys were given time away from their normal classroom lessons to develop their project further into fresh areas. The link between children and teacher, children and specialist, children and workshop and finally specialist and teacher was all important in the creation of an art object which had relevance to an immediate situation. The workshop area in this case, and in subsequent cases, was not used to instigate craft work, but rather to extend the boys' work and stretch their thinking. The basic idea was the major contributing factor, as it should be in all creative activity.

The freedom of the specialist, not tied to a rigid timetable, made it possible to cater for the needs of two individuals outside the class situation. The class teacher, having observed the final results of his early foundational work, also received a sense of satisfaction and realised a deeper trust and respect for Art, a subject which had had little appeal to him before.

Extending this last remark, I would say that in the Middle school situation, the specialist's performance (when acting in a super-numerary capacity) is often an intricate entanglement of roles. It calls for tact and diplomacy when working alongside other staff and with children who, being so involved in their own classroom work (naturally enough), initially fail to see the relevance of another teacher's potential because he is not immediately related to that class or year group. The solution involves a mixture of politics and salesmanship. One of my main, self-inflicted problems was to go all out for the "hard-sell" of my subject and then to find myself inundated with requests for project ideas and advice, a situation which proved difficult at times but convinced me that the ultimate approach was right. To find oneself involved in at least three projects at once, each demanding its own approach, was a hard, but nevertheless a very intriguing and refreshing experience.

One such project involved me with the First Year Group of nine to ten year olds. The theme was "France" It was instigated by the year group's French specialist. I was invited to join the year group on their activity afternoons and initiate Art and Craft work within the context of this theme. I began by conversing with six children of mixed ability extracted for me from the year group by the First Year Head. We began by discussing the project and Art in general. There were certain basic ideas and attitudes I wished to inculcate although my prime aim was to get to know the children, and indeed the age group, which was new to me, and to make sure that they understood my involvement and interest in their work. From what I can remember of the conversation, I have included a grossly condensed and somewhat artificial version here:-

"Miss V. tells me that you are all keen painters. How true is that?"

Philip: *"Yes, I like painting. I did a lot at my last school. I do it at home as well. My Mum gets fed up of seeing me with a pencil in my hand".*

Paul: *"It's best at school though. We have more materials to use and it doesn't matter so much if you make a mess."*

Patricia: *"You shouldn't make a mess really. Not if you paint properly."*

"Can I ask you all what may seem a strange question? Why is it, do you think, that you come to school at all to paint and draw as part of your work?"

Patricia: *"To make the classroom look nice, I suppose."*

Caroline: *"To learn about colours and things."*

Philip: *"So that we can get a good job when we leave school."* (A common enough answer to a question of this nature - especially in this part of the world.)

"Yes, well all these answers are true to a certain extent, but let's try to find some new answers, perhaps ones you haven't thought about before. Supposing you each knew something that no-one else knew. Perhaps you had been out walking alone and you had come across a cat catching a bird or you'd seen the first spring butterfly. If you really wanted to tell someone about this, your parents, say, or a friend, how would you pass on your message? In what way or ways would they be able to find out about this event from you?"

Caroline: *"Just tell them about it. Talk to them, have a conversation."*

"Use words, that's right. How would you tell someone who lives a hundred miles away?"

Patricia: *"You could telephone, if you had one."*

"Suppose you were a reporter on the local newspaper. What would you do then?"

Caroline: *"Write a story about it, like people who write books."*

"Are there any other ways in which you might let other people know what you are thinking about?"

Philip: *"You could paint a picture. You might take a photograph if you had a camera."*

"All right, so there are lots of ways of passing on information to other people. As Philip says, one way might be to paint a picture, or, in other words, tell your story in colours and shapes and patterns. Let's think about our project for a moment. (The word "our" was used deliberately and often). *I'm sure that you already know a great deal about France. Miss M. has spent a great deal of time explaining things to you. Do you like those posters outside in the year space?"*

Paul: *"I like the one of Notre Dame - the big cathedral. It looks golden."*

Philip: *"Miss M. told us that they don't have double decker buses in France."*

Caroline: *"I like the houses with shutters at the windows and the cafés on the pavements."*

(All the children went into great depths about the things that interested them most. Lorraine, up to this point, had said very little. Justine, it was discovered had actually been to France on holiday and was able to tell the others a great deal about the Eiffel Tower and the Arc de Triomphe).

The pictures were large and took time to do. Lorraine, remedial and slow, was still at the X-ray stage of drawing and placed the furniture on the outside walls of her houses, but spent six weeks on her picture. The others spent nearly as long, doing a little each day. I was amazed at such concentrated effort, patience and complete involvement. The pictures oozed hard work.

The outcome was that the class teachers, having noted the work of these six children, passed the paintings around the year group. The effect was staggering to say the least. On a subsequent visit to the first year, I found practically the whole year group with paper and materials trying to emulate the work of my small group of six. Their influence had been absolute.

I found this type of thing happening all over the school. Other teachers and other children wanting to paint, wanting their work to be exciting and successful, demanding increased knowledge asking techniques, seeking honest opinion. To see the brighter and more skilful children helping the less able was quite a revelation.

Much of the work was to me, as a specialist, second hand. It demanded a course of action similar to that of a wireless operator attempting to tune in to a new wavelength every five minutes. Year groups working on such topics as The Elements, The Olympic Games, Transport, Decimal Currency, Food. Individuals or groups of children were involved in personal research into Sailing Ships, Churches, Costume, the Eskimoes and so on, all with a visual statement to make.

1 Graham, aged eleven years constructed a galleon to scale in balsa wood. He displayed considerable skill in pinning and glueing the internal structure of ribs and an aptitude for needlecraft when he stitched the sails. His skill in shipbuilding stayed with him into the fourth year when he made a Viking ship befitting any museum as part of a "Making of the British" project. He was generally a bright boy who set a fine example to his peers, often stopping his own work to help others. He became quite a leader.

2 Catherine, on the other hand, rejected any form of visual expression. When invited to draw, she would immediately burst into tears and express her incompetence. Despite many conversations with her and attempts to reassure her that her abilities were comparable with her colleagues, she only managed to complete one picture in her final year at the school.

3 Andrew, aged twelve, is in my class at present. His reading age is very low and this is reflected in his academic work. Given a quantity of clay at the beginning of the year, he modelled an excellent life-sized bust of a prehistoric man and later followed this up with a clay portrait of Winston Churchill, which possessed a remarkable likeness to the great man.

4 Joseph, aged thirteen, was very poor academically, aggressive by nature and constantly in trouble for his bad behaviour, but when given needle and thread, he would produce work superior to that of any girl. His work was often on display and he undoubtedly derived pleasure and satisfaction from this. (Raymond, one of the boys who made the locust, was in fact the first boy to begin the "boys doing needlework" cult. Despite amusement and leg-pulling from other boys, he determinedly sat in the classroom sewing. It wasn't long before the others took to the idea. The battle had been won.)

5 When the school first opened, Pearl, aged twelve, was immediately fascinated by the new sewing machines. Mrs S., too busy organising her area, did not have time to show Pearl how the machine worked. Instead she gave her the instruction manual and Pearl taught herself. She eventually gave instruction to members of staff - a complete reversal of roles when pupil became teacher.

There are many such examples which illustrate how the values and purposes of Art and Craft education within a Middle school domain are so relevant, indeed dynamic. I do not intend to define the value and role of Art and Craft in education here - many good books do this already. My only misgiving is that teachers undervalue the intuitive, emotional and spiritual aspects of natural development, what Herbert Read describes as *"educating the subconscious mind"*.

It is necessary, in school, to cover all the various aspects of Art, namely the illustrative, the appreciative, the technical and the creative. The latter is, without doubt the key factor. With sensitive handling, the creative imagery produced by a child can be channelled into so many learning situations and the ensuing insight into his personality can be of enormous value to a teacher aware enough to realise the implications. The tendency, however, seems to be towards too much emphasis on diagrammatic illustration, out-and-out technique with the prime emphasis on skills and processes. It would be naïve to say that these should not be taught, but what is the point of learning how to use a lawn mower if there is no lawn to cut? Children's work in this area derives not merely from their obvious abilities in isolation, but through the accumulation of all their energies, be they emotional, intellectual or physical.

There is an enormous respect in schools for creative writing. Teachers will go to great lengths to introduce stimuli of all kinds in order to extract emotive and descriptive words from children. Some fine writing, as I have witnessed, is produced in great quantity. But words, by themselves, are often inadequate and perhaps frustrating, especially for those pupils who lack linguistic fluency. If the same energies were devoted to creative painting or to put it more precisely, to those natural impulses that have been born within every man, then perhaps that instinct would not be dispelled quite so readily at the age of adolescence when it appears that art loses its mantle of respectability and is supplanted by verbal expression.

I now wish to go into detail concerning two major year group projects. One involved work and study of one of the largest and most architecturally beautiful houses of the eighteenth century period, namely Wentworth Woodhouse, near Rotherham, the Great East Front of which is at present a College of Education. The project was organised in collaboration with the college staff and a small group of students. The other was a project entitled "Man and His Materials". The aim here was to visit small firms in the Barnsley area, observe such materials as clay, wood, glass, coal and metal being used in different processes to produce commercial goods and then to use the same or similar materials in school either scientifically or aesthetically. The resultant school work would emphasise the various qualities of the materials and their creative possibilities. I use the word "creative" to envelop scientific discovery as well as aesthetic expression.

Both projects were carried out with the same children. The year group was relatively small, ninety children, so new types of organisation were possible and all areas in and around the year group space were utilised to their fullest extent.

The Wentworth Project

General Aim: To study the Wentworth Area, the House, the Village and their geographical, historical and sociological relationships to one another. The work to be appropriate to twelve to thirteen year old children.

Specific Aim: To explore and discover form, construction, style, age, location and relationship of buildings and areas within Wentworth as a means of achieving certain educational objectives.

Objectives:

1 To increase the children's awareness and enjoyment of their surroundings, people, things indoor and outdoor, by accurate observation of this new environment.

2 To increase their understanding of man-built elements of the landscape.

3 To stimulate growth of children's:-
   a) Critical faculties.
   b) Ability to apply their discoveries and analysis to future projects and subsequently life outside school.

4 To provide opportunity for imaginative and self-expressive work, oral, written and visual.

My task as Head of Year Group was to make several preliminary visits to Wentworth to discuss details of the project with college staff beforehand. I also needed to weigh up all the possibilities. Arrangements were made with local notables including the Headmaster of the village school, who in fact agreed to show us old record books and even cordially invited us to use the school in case of bad weather, the local vicar, who agreed to open the old church (now in a dilapidated state) and put on a bell ringing ceremony in the new church, and the Estate Manager, whose co-operation we needed to allow us to look over the estate, to talk about forestry and to act as guide. Other local people were also consulted. I then co-ordinated all aspects of the project.

As this was my first effort at organising such a project, I was naturally anxious for it to succeed and was therefore dissatisfied until every minor detail had dropped into place. Year group meetings took place so that my colleagues could suggest ideas and methods of organisation. It was important too that advisory staff be encouraged to contribute.

The children were split into mixed ability groups with at least one boy or girl who had potential as a leader. It was also important to give the less able children a certain degree of responsibility. Very careful consideration was given to which children each group contained. Within a year group situation, it is vital that every child is known thoroughly - perhaps more so than in any other kind of grouping.

Several visits were organised in advance and for the purpose of these the children were arranged conveniently into six groups of fifteen, each with a member of staff or students in charge. The groups were as follows:-

Group 1 To study the House interior and the history of the family.

Group 2 To study the exterior of the House, its architecture and immediate grounds.

Group 3 To study the two churches in the village - one eighteenth century and the other twelfth century.

Group 4 To study the village - mainly one long street.

Group 5 To study the wider surroundings of the House, the Estate and the pastoral industries carried out.

Group 6 To study the geography of Wentworth, the various monuments and follies erected by the late family, to seek a relationship between the House and the village, and gain as much information as possible from local people.

Staff and students were allocated to groups according to their individual skills and interests.

One of the college lecturers, an authority on the history of Wentworth and the House, began the project by giving a key lecture to the whole year group. The various rooms along the Great East Front were mentioned, the names of notable members of the Fitzwilliam family were made known, several anecdotes were passed on and slides were shown.

Each child was provided with a map showing the ten mile journey from school to Wentworth, a questionnaire to answer en route, five detailed sheets on the Fitzwilliam family, the House and the rooms inside. Everyone was also provided with writing and drawing materials, and a board and clip. Some children brought cameras.

1st Visit: Groups 1, 2 and 5 tour of the House and grounds at half hour intervals.
Groups 3 and 4 tour of the village, church bell ringing.
Groups 6 visit to small farm owned by local builder.
Groups 1, 2 and 5 alternating between conducted tour of house, walk along terrace and sketching East Front.
Length of visit - 2¼ hours.

2nd Visit: Groups 3, 4, 6 to visit House.
Groups 1, 2, 5 visit to Estate woodyard, through village. Collect samples.

3rd Visit: All groups to begin work on assignments.

Subsequent visits by individual groups in school minibus to reassess, answer new questions, refresh observation.

The main bulk of the work was carried out in school on two afternoons per week, although nothing was rigidly fixed and staff used other periods of class time to carry out written work, painting, model making or display. Latterly, the afternoon timetable was abandoned altogether in a last ditch effort to complete as much of our anticipated work as possible. The whole project was brought to a climax by a selected display in the school's central Display Area. Selection had to take place. There wasn't enough space to house all the work.

The real success of the adventure may never really be known. There was no doubt that the children, coming from a mining community into a rural setting were deeply impressed by the splendour of such a magnificent House, its chandeliers, mirrors, libraries, wall decorations, pillars and so on. Simply to be there was experience enough.

It would be pertinent to observe a few examples:

1 David, aged fifteen, shy, introverted, quiet to the point of being silent, was greatly impressed by the stone balustrade around the edge of the roof along the Great East Front. He moved along the 600ft. length of the building sketching the different skyline shapes. Back at school, his attempts to recreate his sketches in pen and ink failed. I helped him by suggesting that his drawings might be better as silhouettes either inked in or even cut out of black paper. He was pleased with his first new attempt and continued to produce dozens of these. Any attempt on my part to suggest a change of approach or something different met with blank rejection. He had found something that was pleasing to him. On the wall, the silhouettes showed up in a remarkably striking manner almost echoing the building itself.

2 Stephen and Jeffrey usually spent most of their class time gossiping and being generally lazy. It was quite a revelation to find them unusually engrossed in the making of a model of the huge portico, Corinthian columns and all, from card, wood and polyfilla. Although I kept a distant eye on them working out in the year space, they needed little help and completed a lifelike model which we photographed. Stephen has left school now. His model has pride of place at home. His parents helped to transport it home safetly.

3 Neil, aged thirteen, an asthma sufferer who found enormous difficulties in living a normal life, was one of those relatively few children who showed a rare talent for drawing, especially portraits. His picture, a large, shaded pencil drawing, illustrated the dream he had had about Wentworth. The drawing contained several elements closely interrelated and overlapping. These included the House, the marble statues inside, the village church spire showing above the trees, a domed folly and the Fitzwilliam coat-of-arms. It had immediate appeal to the other children. An on the spot lesson ensued, as I used Neil's picture as a lead into the History of Art and the Surrealist Painters. Wentworth, naturally presented many such opportunities to discuss Art and Architecture. Fortunately, the school library is well stocked with books on both subjects.

Man and his materials

For this project, the general weekly timetable was abandoned for the whole of the first week so that all the visits could be made. This was essential so that work could begin immediately visits to firms were over.

Visits to the following industrial works were arranged.

1 The Coalite Coke and Chemical Plant nearby (coal, chemicals). A high proportion of the children's fathers work here.
2 The local colliery brickyard (clay).
3 Glass Works, five miles away (glass).
4 Steel Works, six miles away (metal and machinery).
5 Shoddy Mill, six miles away (fabrics).
6 Pipe Works, eight miles away (stoneware clay).
7 Motor Dismantlers, local (scrap metal).
8 Wood Yard, ten miles away (various timbers).
9 Local woods and plantations (timber, natural science).
10 West Riding Environmental Studies Centre (farming, animals).
11 Film and lecture at the school by local newspaper PRO (paper and printing).

On this occasion, the children were given complete freedom of choice as to which visits they wished to make. The criteria for the choice were (a) the materials they most wanted to work in and (b) two visits each, plus the Coalite Plant and the lecture on production of newspapers.

My first expectation was that all the children would eagerly seize the opportunity to visit the glass and steel works, seemingly the most exciting of all the visits arranged.

The majority of children, however, asked to visit the school farm and the woods. Hasty negotiations took place between myself and the children in attempts to balance the groups. Second and third choices were made which solved the problem.

Again, the task of contacting the various firms and arranging the visits was my main occupation. I must say that the amount of co-operation was delightfully encouraging. If I may jump a paragraph or two, one firm actually laid on tea and biscuits for the children and provided them with leaflets and brochures.

Being an artist, I arranged six groups and named them Red, Orange, Yellow, Green, Blue and Purple. Mathematics and Art are so easily reconcilable.

Group	1st Visit	2nd Visit	
Red	Brickyard Thursday 14th 2.00 p.m. On Foot	Pipeworks Wednesday 20th 2.00 p.m. By Bus	Clay
Orange	Glassworks Friday 15th 2.00 p.m. School Mini Bus	Pipeworks Wednesday 20th 2.00 p.m. By Bus	Glass Clay
Yellow	Woods Tuesday 12th 1.30 p.m. School Mini Bus	Environmental Studies Centre Thursday 28th School Mini Bus	Timber Soil etc.
Green	Steelworks Wednesday 13th 1.30 p.m. By Bus	Brickyard Thursday 14th 2.00 p.m. On Foot	Metal Clay
Blue	Steelworks Wednesday 13th 1.30 p.m. By Bus	Scrap Yard Thursday 14th 11.00 a.m. School Mini Bus	Metal
Purple	Shoddy Mill Wednesday 13th 1.30 p.m. School Mini Bus	Wood Yard Tuesday 19th 2.00 p.m. School Mini Bus	Fabrics Fibres

All groups to Coalite Plant Monday 11th 10.00 a.m.-3.45 p.m.
All groups film/lecture "How a Newspaper is Made" Tuesday 10th 10.00 a.m.

Aims:

1 To use the local environment in a fresh way following on from the aims and objectives of the Wentworth Project.

2 To discover fresh outlets and possibilities for further school projects.

3 To provide a six weeks' intensive working atmosphere.

4 To encourage staff to work closely together as a team providing a blanket of information and guidance.

5 To force the children deliberately into a situation whereby they would need to seek help, advice and information from whichever member of staff could provide it. No one member of staff was in charge of any group. Staff simply went on the visits they most fancied.

6 To work in a practical rather than theoretical way. Each child was, however, expected to write an account of his visits and produce an informative booklet about his chosen material.

7 To use the chosen materials intelligently through a discovered knowledge of their various properties.

8 To use the year group areas and specialist rooms to their maximum extent.

Spaces Used:

1 The fourth year group classrooms
2 The year group space
3 The Science Area
4 The Workshop
5 The Home Economics Area
6 The Library and Audio Visual Aids

The total cost of the journeys was no more than 15p per child. The variety of work produced was most encouraging, highly creative and totally absorbing.

Peter, aged thirteen, had had little interest in school work. He could not read, was ridiculed by his peers, had enormous difficulties at home. His mother, the driving force in the family, had died the previous year. His trust in one member of staff, individual attention, a six week's course in outdoor pursuits organised within the year group, and more, helped Peter with his reading and enabled him to become more socially acceptable. He turned out to have an enormous sense of humour. As part of the "Man and His Materials Project", he not only carried out various experiments on coal - heating the coal in a bunsen burner and extracting tars etc., - but also constructed a blown glass mobile, each shape containing brightly coloured liquids. The mobile was placed in the year space in order to catch the sunlight from the window.

Work produced included:

Glass blown sculpture
Metal sculpture - copper, steel and aluminium
Pottery - earthenware and stoneware
Beaten copper work
Wood turning on the workshop lathe

Functional objects in wood and needlecrafts
Fabric collage
Ceramic sculpture
Etching and various forms of printmaking including silkscreen
Germination and propagation of seeds and plants
Wood carving
Experiments with glaze and other ceramic materials
Batique work

All the case studies and examples here only go part way to explaining the true nature or value of the creative work that can be carried out in a Middle school situation, but they are perhaps vivid enough to illustrate some of the work that can be done with mixed ability groups and my earlier remarks on the potentiality of Art and Craft in education. Further details of the structure and organisation of topics, projects, individual assignments and group work are given elsewhere in this book[1] and these will help to put my examples and remarks into a more coherent and broader context.

It is important, however, to re-iterate the aims and philosophy upon which such creative work is based lest the reader assume that work of this kind arrives like the housemartin - by sheer instinct. No "theme" teaching can really be effective without carefully detailed pre-planning. Within this process, the role of each member of staff, whether member of the year group team or "adviser", must be carefully considered. Much discussion is needed and all aspects of organisation and structure require total and absolute agreement. To be able to know and rely on the fact that the initial ideas, impetus and aspirations one has for a project are shared by other members of the team is reassuring. It is useful to know also that in addition to the knowledge which other teachers possess through their obvious specialisms, they have other knowledge, expertise or experience to offer - a fact which brings me back to my point about "mixed ability teachers". One hopes that the children will also recognise and gain this knowledge and use it to advantage. The rapport thus established between all the members of the alliance, internal or external, is a key factor and one that must not be lightly dismissed.

Returning to the quotation from Marion Richardson, I must stress that the bandwaggon cult of *"free expression"* is not one that I totally subscribe to in any literal sense. Work is not *"free expression"*

as generally understood. It certainly doesn't mean *"please yourself"*.
The belief that it does stems from a lack of understanding and fear
about what to say to a child when he brings out his paintings and
asks for help. It is an approach which leads merely to unconscious
imitation, shallow thinking and feelingless content. *"Free expression"*
is a disciplined activity in which, perhaps surprisingly to some, the
teacher's own imaginative gifts play a very important part. The good
"art teacher" will always take his children's drawings completely
seriously. All children are eager to create visually. Individual
differences do exist. The bright child, like Graham (see page 99) or
his friend Glynn who painted the stable block at Wentworth in such
fine detail that every stone was different have good background
knowledge, can be channelled, asked to do further research and will
accept advice easily and quickly. At the other end of the scale, the
slow learner, usually with one single idea, shallow, lacking in breadth
of understanding, eager to jump in with both feet before being really
certain, not appreciative of all the facts or skills required to carry
out the work, nevertheless still has some valid point to make and
should be helped to produce his best or learn something new or
take stock or gain satisfaction.

Art is a dynamic force within our society. It ought to be such in our
schools too. A much better understanding of the true value of Art
and Craft as a necessary and vital part of a child's total educational
development is now more apparent, but perhaps all the implications
have yet to be fully appreciated.

*"You think of things as they are and ask 'Why'? I dream of things
that never were and say 'Why not'?*

Reference

1 See Chapter 6.

Bibliography

Bassett, G.W., Each One is Different: Teaching for Individual Differences in the Primary School (Australian Council for Educational Research 1968).
Read, Herbert, Education Through Art (Faber 1958).
Schools Council, Children's Growth through Creative Experience (Reinhold 1974 1974).
Schools Council Working Paper No. 42, Education in the Middle Years (Methuen Educational).
Thelen, H.A., Classroom Grouping for Teachability (Wiley 1967).

Chapter 7
The Humanities

D.L. Steels

To be able to identify with and relate to a group is a common human experience in which we all require to have had some success. This phenomenon is important in the development of young people and has to be meaningful to them. Before the formation of mixed ability groups, this identity was given to them in a cruel manner, which labelled some with inferior titles. Confidence, will-power and a sense of purpose in life were often shattered by the category into which they were placed. Society was divided. Some were prevented from enjoying experiences which might contribute to the full growth of the individual.

The children were brought up in the confines of a narrow community, which was egocentric, and therefore they had little on which to base comparison and standard. Many children talked about adventure in terms of travelling on the back of uncle's motor-cycle six or seven miles to a similar village. Only the privileged few had real experience of different modes of life, and these tended to be in the two top streams. What a wealth of opportunity our kids were missing.

Education seemed also to be a fragmented affair, both in subject areas and in the content within those areas, giving our children little possibility of attaining an understanding and connection with the ideals, ideas and concepts of the programme offered them. They were having to establish relationships with different members of staff who had different approaches and temperaments to which the child had constantly to adjust, in many cases spending more time in so doing than in concentrating on the subject. One such first form group had no less than fourteen different members of staff in one week. Clearly the traumatic experience of moving from the Junior school was enough without this. We felt that we had to have some continuity in order to help these youngsters to adapt to their new environment, so that the transfer would be smooth, causing less worry and trouble to them. It was felt that the education of the individual should be a continuous process and therefore it was necessary to have consultations with and also to visit the five contributory Junior schools.

Staff conferences and courses on integrated studies were taking place in which these and other considerations were discussed. Not always was there agreement on the points brought up but later it was found that the process of covering common ground together tended to clarify our thinking. The act of learning was one to which the staff readily subjected themselves, acting as guinea-pigs to any teacher brave enough to give them the stimulus to perform. These were indeed happy times as well as fruitful ones and helped in no small way to weld together the participants in a way which resulted in untold benefits for the children within the school. In addition to our internal in-service training many teachers were strongly influenced by experiences afforded them by a variety of courses run by the West Riding Education Advisory Staff. Here teachers found themselves examining and researching in practical ways the possibilities of education, the process of learning, and the joy, enthusiasm and obvious abandon with which these tasks were undertaken posed for them many questions which had to be answered within the school situation.

Some reforms had to take place, for in those days we thought that it was going to be difficult to establish the principles and philosophy that had become the basis of the new direction in which the staff wished to go. Within the existing framework prototype schemes were tried out which enabled us to meet and discuss the problems and developments of such a course. In one such experiment, fifteen members of staff were directly involved, although the class of thirty children were under the direction or guidance of one member of staff - an artist. This situation could not continue, but it helped us to look at various points which required careful consideration. We were convinced that a thematic approach was best with the emphasis on the individual child's acceptance of a major responsibility for the way he would go and the tools he would use in order to solve and research the problems that he had set himself. This however did not come through as clearly as I have just stated it but evolved gradually from the various schemes which we tried.

The tasks set had diverse solutions. What was pertinent and obvious to one individual was shunned and discarded by another. The crucial factor was that the solution of any problem or task researched should help to develop the full potential of the individual. This possibility in the range of the work meant that the teacher had to have support from colleagues who had specialist knowledge in particular areas. The specialist had to be readily available or indeed had to be involved in the planning conferences which were necessary. Early but crude team teaching was born and timetabled. Motivation appeared to come from the interests of the individual backed by the support of his fellow researchers and by a team of synpathetic staff. This led him from the unknown but in this process he made requests for help which were extending the teacher far beyond his own knowledge. The finding out became a joint adventure of pupil and teacher from which grew the mutual respect that this sytem must have. The pupil was involved in the use of the library, the environment, the community, experts (many of whom were not teachers), films, magazines, newspapers, television, radio, visits, and was spurred on primarily by the excitement of establishing for himself a task and researching this to his personal satisfaction, but all the time he was being extended to his full potential by his teacher.

The teacher was a member of a team; he concerned himself with the development of the child; he was a consultant and friend, a director and an authority, a ways and means man, and a person who was sought out by pupils and staff for advice. He was no longer in a little box in isolation, where he was the ultimate authority; he now had to change his role to fit in with the new philosophy. This was a gradual process - a process which was nowhere near complete. Many accepted and welcomed the situation; others perhaps were uncertain and continued to teach as they always had. This transference from being the planner, the instructor, the disciplinarian in his small domain, to the more demanding and stimulating test of the new situation, was difficult to make. On many of the teachers' courses the natural urge and desire was to work in areas in which the individual felt secure, although this taught them little about the learning situation.

Many teachers and students entering this form of work feel that it is only necessary to establish the initial motivation and then you can sit back and admire the house being built. They seem to set up a barrier between themselves and the children and if this exists then the system collapses. Or else they find themselves being inundated by various requests for help with which, through lack of planning, they cannot cope. The running of our Humanities Course together with mixed ability grouping demands constant planning and preparation, forecasting demands and having available materials and resources. It means extending the various abilities within the group, becoming aware and concerned about the work of individuals, channelling the child's work in such a way as to use his known interests, as well as to attack and remedy his weaknesses. This is a demanding job for the teacher in wrestling with which he will find that his methods and philosophy will gradually change and, we trust, improve.

During this period we referred to the work as being a seed which is planted in all types of soil. The seed sends out roots and begins to grow. For this growth it requires food and water but eventually it produces a stem or trunk from which spring the branches and side shoots. On these grow the leaves which may fall to the ground and are of no further use except that they then create excellent nourishment for the roots. The initial stimulus or idea was the seed which was sown in the ground - the individual material within the group. The roots are the technical abilities each child could possess and these must be improved as they will govern the quality of the resultant plant. The fertilising of these ideas, the support of the young sapling, the nurturing of the growth, the adding of the right ingredients at the correct time will be the teachers' responsibility. The trunk is the core knowledge possessed and acquired whilst the branches and shoots are the individual research and pathways of thought that each will follow.

The staff working along these lines find that the demands made upon them are varied, but that these demands come from the child to the teacher. This makes the conversation between the child and the teacher that much more real and meaningful and a delight to the teacher since he knows that the child is listening because he himself made the initial request. Similarly it is important that the child sees that the teacher is willing to carry out the same tasks as he is working at both in and out of lesson time. The learning process becomes a joint venture. With some children the teacher may have to supply and nurture the root growth for most of the time, in order to help the child to see success and therefore attain a sense of achievement. The task to be accomplished by teacher and child may be a specific technical point or a matter of standard or presentation or of endurance or perseverance with the task or the ability to collate information. The teacher is concerning himself with every child individually, thus increasing the volume of work and preparation which is necessary to establish his relationships and help the total learning situation.

The resultant product is the formation of a balanced growth; in techniques acquired, in formation of character and personality, in the form and shape of thinking, in understanding, in the process of learning and in the accomplishment of a task in its entirety. The body of knowledge gained by each child is different; the way to that knowledge is much more important and, coupled with this, what has happened to that child on the route.

The Humanities programme at Northcliffe occupies between two-fifths and one third of the total timetable, made up of whole mornings or afternoons, which gives us the flexibility to manoeuvre in order to create our programme. Even with this arrangement staff still complain that the time allowed is not enough, which suggests many things, the least of which is that they enjoy the privilege of working with the mixed ability groups in this way.

The team teaching is completely blocked across each year group without any children being excluded. Amongst other advantages, this enables us to deal with any disciplinary problems in a unique way. We believe that these problems arise through clashes of personality either between teacher and child or between one child and another; they also appear through the influences children exercise on each other. Our remedy is simple and in the main it works. Eight groups are working along the same lines and so we attempt to place any child who presents disciplinary problems into another situation with another teacher and another group of pupils. Care must be taken in doing this, of course, even to attempting to ensure that the child should suggest or at least agree to the change.

The Humanities programme is block time-tabled completely across the eight mixed ability forms. Thus 240 pupils are working in the Humanities with a team of eight staff. The team is a balanced group of teachers usually covering the four subjects which we decided we would include in our scheme. Our work is firmly based on a thematic approach which incorporates English, History, Geography, and Moral and Social Studies.

The freedom of choice enjoyed by the child and the resultant drive to learn which comes from within him, along with the relationships fostered by the members of staff, who seeing their pupils for a third of the week are able to know them more intimately, establish a method of working which will help and persuade the child to learn. In this form of learning, as in all methods, there is, of course, room for the child to appear fully occupied, to produce work in quantity and yet not be fully engaged in the learning process. This is where the expertise, foresight, and planning of the teacher takes over. He has at his command a comprehensive guide or syllabus to which he and the child can refer for the development of individual study. The tools to be used in the extension of any idea are also numerous. The teacher and, more particularly, the child, together create a need for the use of such tools. Hence learning begins from the urge and willingness of the child because the reasons for learning come from him. He is the instigator and as such possesses the desire to complete his task no matter what it entails. It is towards the finding of such keys to unlock the doors that the team is constantly striving.

In many instances the tools may be outside the immediate area of the four disciplines. In these cases the teacher may seek advice from another specialist or request him to discuss the problem with the child. Such help is always granted. Thus true integration is achieved with a merging of the disciplines, and not the fragmented teaching of the separate subjects.

During an English lesson of a traditional kind the teacher had spent a good deal of time in dealing with paragraphs and had been successful in making the children aware and confident in the use of them. The following week the class had progressed to another technique and Eric, an above average boy, completed some writing. The teacher after seeing it asked Eric where his paragraphs were. *"Oh! I thought we did them last week - I didn't know that we were doing them again this week."*

There are many such stories that could be told from other areas of the curriculum, which illustrate the problem of relating learning to practical application. This sort of thing is happening all the time. It is our aim to attempt to promote, as well as we possibly can, the interrelation of the various skills and techniques acquired by the child in whatever learning situation he may choose. Historical studies merge into English or Moral studies. There is no divorce of one discipline from another for each is equally important to the other. They are married and become a concerted unit working for the benefit of the individual and the integrity of the mixed ability group. They are merely tools to accomplish a task. Each child is able to find an interest and thus to make a valuable contribution to the whole development of the course and to the other children in the group. The ideas and knowledge of those of least ability also are extended by the group, thus giving to the instigator a boost to his confidence. The finished product is important, but the processes by which the child progresses to that end result are far more important as contributory factors in the development of his full potential. To support this development he requires the friendship and guidance of his peers and the sympathy and understanding of his teacher, who will answer his call for help at any time.

The Humanities syllabus for our fourth and fifth years was strongly influenced by the School Council Humanities Curriculum Project, but, although we have used their material, we have adapted it to meet our own needs. We do not, for example, timetable discussion time within our Humanities programme, but feel that the discussion which obviously will arise should do so spontaneously from the interested parties - then we have a real discussion with a real purpose.

We submitted our syllabus to the Joint Matriculation Board and to the West Yorkshire and Lindsey Regional Examinations Board for consideration for GCE "O" level and CSE qualification under a Mode 3 assessment, with grades to be given and determined separately for the four subjects principally involved in the project, English, Geography, History, Moral Education.

We expected, because of certain precedents, that the CSE would readily accept it, but we had considerable doubt about its being accepted by the JMB for GCE "O" level. We need not have worried, for at the top level conferences which ensued the Board displayed sympathy to our request. They asked for specimens of the work that we might submit for assessment. These were sent to the Board. They suggested, after looking at this work, that perhaps we might be subjecting our children to a more rigorous and strenuous two year course than the conventional "O" level course and asked us whether this was really our intention. Thus the discussions proceeded with advice and guidance being offered through these initial stages and the Board continuing to be helpful. We felt secure with this backing and in no small way this encouraged and comforted us in this most trying period. We had always believed that what we were doing for our children was the right thing, but now, if they wished, they were able to aim at qualifications that the outside world would recognise and therefore to compete on equal terms with other youngsters. A criticism is levelled at the "O" level boards that they tend to stifle real progress in learning and that the programmes that they demand are so rigid that teaching becomes an imparting of knowledge and fact without reference to other major educational considerations. We found none of this.

We accepted certification in the four subject areas to give our children currency for the Rat Race of modern society, but would have been happier with just four grades in the Humanities for this would have enabled us to develop our course without the restrictions which we now find upon us. One of the biggest drawbacks to the scheme as it works at the moment is that one child may do a huge volume of work in two fields and only obtain two qualifications whilst another may spread into all four areas, doing no more work and yet receive twice as many qualifications. This of course becomes a major teaching point since we must make sure that each capable child covers all four areas. This is a responsibility which we pass on to the pupil and in this respect it adds to the course.

Our approach is through a series of themes from which the child produces his own study, but we always include a certain amount of core work which is completed by all students. Here is our choice of topics or themes as it stands at the moment.

Term 1
1 British Industry (Introduced at Easter of the third year)
Term 2
2 The Challenge of the Unstable Earth (Initially at this point we dealt with Relationships between the Sexes)
3 War and Society
Term 3
4 Education
5 The Family
Term 4
6 Law and Order
7 People and Work
Term 5
8 The Community in which we live ⎫   Field Work and Community
9 Our Environment   ⎬   Service in addition to
Term 6   ⎭   writing and discussion.
10 Own choice of theme and final dissertations

The first and last occupy a full term's work whilst the others have only half of this time. This was arranged deliberately for in the early stages certain fundamental skills and techniques have to be dealt with in great detail in order to establish within the child the right approach by which research of the nature expected can be achieved, whilst in the latter stages the choice is entirely the individual's and, so that he may utilise as many of the techniques acquired throughout the course as possible, he is given that valuable commodity - time. During this final term each pupil has to complete four dissertations. These are based on a subject area of the course and may take a full day to complete. While they are writing these, they are permitted to bring into the room any resource material but must acknowledge quotations.

From the above themes I choose "The Family" as my example of the syllabus. In this one all the four contributory disciplines are involved, whereas in some of the others this is not possible. This is a condensed version to conserve space.

The Family

Issues for discussion, writing and research:

The average British Family: The problems of a house-bound wife; Conflict between school and home; Effects of women at work; Problems of the adolescent in the family; Home management and budgeting; Child-rearing and discipline; Adoption.

Families in different parts of the world: Western, Christian families; Jewish and others; Family life in primitive cultures.

The Family in Britain: The immediate and extended family; The autonomy of the family; What do you expect from marriage and family life?

The Family as an economic unit: Man as the breadwinner; Contributions by children to the family coffers; Housing, urban and rural.

The Family as a social unit: The net-work of relations; Health - a free nurse; Neighbours; Social and emotional stability.

So it goes on under the main headings:- The Family and Christianity; The uni-nuclear and multi-nuclear family; Changes in family structure; Personal relationships; Childhood; Youth; Old Age.

This part of our syllabus covers a period of six or seven weeks and from this it will be apparent that this is not intended as a list of work to be completed but is merely a guide to the possibilities that this particular theme offers. In fact in any group working in the Humanities it is conceivable that each of these studies could be in progress, or the entire group could be involved in completing one of them, or small groups could be carrying out research together on several of them.

The weekly team conference (which is time-tabled) is essential in maintaining and sustaining the course and it needs to be supported by extra untimetabled conferences. At these, planning of a preliminary nature takes place long before the work is to be commenced and is followed by more detailed discussion on the course. Are we to make any alterations in content or application? What problems do we foresee? We feel that it is vital to vary any presentation of material and any organisation in order that the method does not become stereotyped and thus lack the necessary vitality which is of paramount importance to the course. How are we to use the specialist knowledge of the staff? I give but a few of the issues which can arise in our meetings. Having then received as it were a directive from my team I, as leader, then proceed to produce a timetable in order to provide a structure within which further detailed planning can take place.

For a new school year commencing in September the initial planning starts in early June with a decision on the types and names of films to be shown. These are then ordered for the ensuing year. The past year is reviewed in detail and any major amendments made to our programme whether they are in content or in application.

Of the developments which have taken place in the last few years one of the major ones is the establishing of the team situation. We had always claimed that it existed but in effect it only functioned for specific purposes and these were only spasmodic. In those early days the team existed in the minds of the staff and was used well by them, but the children had little idea about the specialist field of any particular member of the team. Nothing had been created in the minds of the children which would help this situation. In some way we had to embark on a major advertising campaign.

This we attempted to do in various ways. The first attempt was made during the War and Society theme when we decided to have a teach-in on Vietnam. This was intended to be the initial stimulus for a mini-study in which all the children would be involved. In this the major contributor was the geographer who dealt with the position of Vietnam, the relief, the vegetation, the terrain, the social and economic life of the people and various other physical and natural phenomena of the country. For this he had produced a wealth of resource material so that the children would be able to follow their own chosen programmes. He used overhead projector slides and the epidiascope with pictures as well as large maps of the area. The geographer had arrived in the minds of those children and from then on was sought out to help with a range of relevant problems by direct requests. In similar ways the other specialists were introduced to, accepted and subsequently manipulated by the people who mattered - the children.

Obviously, to support such a scheme we had to have a resource centre. In the early stages of the course because of the pressures of the work we were living from hand to mouth. We have to have material of all types and at all levels in order to cope with the mixed ability groups. We have to extend the brightest and yet cater for the needs of the remainder. The development of a resources centre is progressing slowly for with a full teaching commitment time is the drawback. However, because we have created situations and conditions which allowed a member of staff to spend some time on the arduous task of collecting and storing resource materials, we are eventually building up a very good centre.

The other vital factor in the shortage of material was lack of cash. We had the Schools' Council Humanities packs on War and Society, Relationships between the Sexes, Education and The Family. To these we have recently added Living in Cities which seems to have some relevance for the majority of our themes. Our most recent additions of material to the resources centre have been the results of our attempts to create units of work on particular areas of study within the theme. So far we have met with limited success and intend to review and develop these as and when the time permits. To explain what is happening in this sector would take a great deal of time but our aim is to produce a simple but effective system not just for the use of the staff but in order that the children can feel secure and at ease in using it themselves. It is beginning to happen.

With the flexibility of our syllabus, the utilisation of the different disciplines and the growth of the philosophy of the school, which is closely connected with the method of working within the Humanities, we have more than a head start in catering for the mixed ability groups. All the children within the group are following the same course, but at their own level and at their own speed. The development of their study being a personal one is more meaningful to them and any ensuing teaching is devised to cater for the individual's needs. At the same time each child has the support and encouragement of fellows who are following parallel studies. Information found is passed on or discussed so that a greater understanding follows, for what is relevant to one is not necessarily relevant to another. Indeed in our Humanities rooms there can be a great deal of purposeful movement, for material may be found on the overhead projectors (sometimes produced by the teacher but at other times produced by one of the children), on the slide projector (again material commercially produced or else the result of some past student's work), on the tape-recorder, in the resource room, in the library, or even from some visitor or teacher who is available at that time. Education becomes a joint venture which cuts across the ability range as do the recreational activities of these children.

The element of competition is taken out of the performance, for the school policy of non-examination and its commitment to the Mode 3 method of continuous assessment is such that the only way in which performance is considered is through the actual progress that each individual makes. A good deal of this cannot be measured by conventional means, for we are not just expecting the technical ability of the child to improve in a certain discipline, but are equally concerned with his social adjustments and the development of the more desirable traits of a stable character. We aim, for example, by our own tolerance to enable the children to show similar tolerance in their relations with others.

Thus by the responses which occur in the mixed ability group the children are able to assimilate the right experiences which one ability group can give to another, indeed to discuss or reject any points which arise which they find not acceptable to them. This perhaps is an adaptation of the valuable work performed by Bill Marshall at Childscourt and other establishments with which he was concerned, work which was of course strongly influenced by his short experience at Summerhill.

Another valuable feature of our scheme is that the children are never looked upon as fitting into any particular ability group and suffer less from feelings of inferiority than they would if they had been clearly categorised. Some of the children of lesser ability are amongst the most prolific researchers and produce a wealth of experience for the benefit of the entire group. To see and hear one of these children holding his own in a discussion or explaining a point on how to use a camera or tape-recorder is a joy for the beholder and the subsequent boost to that child's confidence is unequalled in any other situation. Having been accepted in that situation he then becomes the authority on that subject and his advice and counsel is requested time and time again.

The groups that are formed in the Humanities course are not based deliberately on a mixing of abilities but are friendship groups. In these it is more than possible that a good range of ability will be found. Children belonging to such a group will be working at their own pace and level, with the obvious advice and help that comes from good friends. This is proved from the number of discussions and, at times, arguments that occur in the children's leisure time.

What appears to emerge from the work of these groups is a desire to know. It is manifested within the individual in the form of requests for help both to friends and to the teacher. Unfortunately this appears at a late stage in some of the children and we are at the moment examining this point to see if, in some way, we may speed up its development.

Presentation of material is another technique which is enhanced in the mixed ability group situation, for there is available in any group a better selection of material for display. The children are also encouraged to experiment and aim at a high standard of presentation by the examples which are set by the displays in the Humanities rooms.

Perhaps the most serious problem which teachers find in entering this situation is that when it is working it appears so easy and seems to their mind to require little or no preparation. They are ill-equipped to tackle this unless they are sympathetic to the methods being used. Some find great difficulty too in concerning themselves with the individual because they have always thought of teaching a class as a whole and of course in the mixed ability situation this method is only occasionally used. When it is used, the follow up work has to provide enough scope for all the abilities, giving each child the opportunity to understand and develop the material with which he is confronted at his own pace and level.

It was once said of the Windmill Theatre that it never closed. This is also true of Northcliffe for we have an extension of the day on four evenings in the week. This we refer to as The Third Session. The success of this is shown by the large number of children who attend for social, cultural, recreational and educational reasons. The Humanities contribute on all four evenings in some form or another. It is surprising how the reluctant ones will return in order to do a specific task such as editing a tape recording or putting up a display of work - usually their own. I heard one such boy say, as he was mounting a piece of his work, *"When this goes on the wall it will be the first time that anything of mine has been up."* Surely this did something for this lad! The Humanities room is open so that the children can do their homework under suitable conditions, with all the resources available and the attendance of one or more of the staff. We have special evenings when we may view a television programme together and then have a discussion about it. Visiting speakers attend and one such occasion that I remember particularly was the visit of Dorothy Hyman, the British international athlete. What an evening this was, as the children were able to rub shoulders with one of the greatest sprinters this country has produced. We use our local community as much as possible and we have had evening visits from JPs, a local pigeon fancier, a senior probation officer, an angler, a nurse, a doctor, a policeman (one of our old boys), a miner, a farmer, a housewife, a walker who had just completed The Pennine Way walk, a Trade Union representative, an unemployed person and many other people of different religions, cultures and ways of life. The evening film is always well attended, whilst numerous excursions are well supported. In this way we extend the education of all our children as well as creating interests and activities to help them grow in confidence and stature so that they may be that much better equipped to fulfil their future lives.

It would be wrong of me to conclude this case study of the Humanities course without a word about the staff who form an almost irreplaceable unit in its development and function. They above all have shown their belief in the scheme by displaying so much dedication, both in time and energy, that one wonders how they are able to maintain it. Not a thing is too much trouble to them. Requests from the children or other members of staff are equally attended to without the customary grumbles and grouses. The Humanities programme and the mixed ability groupings have evolved jointly with the philosophy of the school, bringing an awareness of a common purpose in the educating of our youngsters. It is this perhaps which has kept them going. Consider for one moment their work load. The marking of the completed study, the planning and preparation for the future one and the actual working on the present one, with discussions and consideration of some major issue that has been brought to the notice of the team by one of its members. You might say this is not different from the work load of a teacher of a conventional subject. It should not be, but when you are a member of a team then the team carries on playing sometimes when you do not wish to play, and as we have only eight members of our teaching team we cannot afford the luxury of a passenger because the game is with the future of 240 children.

Perhaps they are spurred on in their efforts by the exciting thought of the future extensions to our existing building. These are of a major nature costing close on one million pounds and include a purpose built integrated unit for the use of the Humanities. Although this appears to be in the distant future, the team have had discussions on its usage and the methods that it will enable us to employ. During our new theme, for example, which we introduced this year to our fourth form, The Challenge of the Unstable Earth, we decided on an options scheme and this worked so well that it is thought that some development of this idea may be tried. We have spoken of the possibility of relieving a member of the team from his teaching commitment in order to prepare a unit for use in some subsequent week. This of course would be an internal arrangement and care would be taken that the children did not suffer. Another solution might be to allow the children to vote with their feet by presenting them with a weekly programme so that they may decide their own involvement in whatever direction they choose. There must, however, be a range of choices available to them so that a real decision can be made. Self-discipline, self-regulation, self-concern and self-motivation will also have to be instilled and cultivated within the child. This will be backed by a tutorial system with, we believe, a weekly meeting of the group. A good many of these techniques are being tried out long before we enter the new building.

All the time we are striving to improve the value of the course to the child. We are making adjustments, performing permutations with the staff in order to obtain cross-fertilisation and attempting to make our material capable of being used by all the children of whatever ability.

Since the introduction of the mixed ability groupings completely throughout the school, the major reform of the timetable and the introduction of the Humanities programme we have seen a stable situation established. There is a liaison between child and child, child and teacher, teacher and teacher, and teacher and parent which we never had before. We are constantly examining our priorities within the educational field and adjusting these to the needs of our children. What we teach and how we teach mixed ability groups is one of the main issues for any teacher to examine, for a *"watered down"* course similar to their own schooling does not work. A firm belief in what you are doing is essential and a display of obvious enthusiasm for the work by the teacher. We believe that our Humanities course is on the right road but it is only one of the many possible solutions to the problem of educating our youngsters.

Chapter 8
English and Drama

B. Liddington

Teachers of English, especially those coming new to the profession, might justifiably find themselves confused and unsure of what exactly they are supposed to do with their classes, since, in English above all, a radical transformation has come about in both content and style of teaching, over the last ten years. From being the most rigidly structured of all the subjects - certainly the easiest to teach (I have even heard it advocated that English teachers should be paid on a lower scale than others), English has now become arguably the least structured and most difficult to teach (at least to teach at all well).

The reasons for this are threefold. Firstly, the programmed course, strongly biased in favour of easily assessable grammatical exactness has been almost totally superseded by the more imaginatively based, creative, Holbrook style of teaching, drawing extensively on language in all its forms as they exist within and around the pupil. Secondly, and related to the previous point, English teaching has become less formal and more concerned with relationships between pupil and community, pupil and teacher, pupil and pupil, and the demands of this, often more abstract and tenuous, are proportionately harder to meet. Thirdly, when this situation is still further "complicated" by the introduction of unstreamed classes, thus removing the final structure of curriculum - according-to-ability (that is, Shakespeare for the "A" stream, Jack-and-Jill for the "D's"), one is left in what can charitably be termed a vacuum. Certainly, the type of preparation I underwent during my post-graduate Education course has been of little help - I have never had recourse to any of the "situations" anticipated then, and a lesson comparing two poems of W.B. Yeats *"for a fourth year 'A' stream"* remains untouched in my Certificate of Education folder.

Given these initial difficulties, what then can the Head of English and his Department do to ensure that the basic demand for literacy and a reasonable oral standard are met, since for all the changes at the "production" end, the needs of the consumer remain unchanged.

I have first and foremost laid stress upon the need for extensive and catholic reading at all levels of ability, and made this the core of the English teaching at Northcliffe. This gives a much needed core to the area of study, and concentrates energies on possibly the most worthwhile and profitable area of English. There is also the added bonus that, if the habit of reading is firmly established at school, it may continue into the post-school years and later life. A well selected book, be it for the child's own personal reading, for a class reader or for the teacher to read to the class, can and will appeal to all tastes and abilities at one and the same time. At best, the concept of work will be forgotten - pushed into the background by the sheer enjoyment to be had from reading a good book (a criterion I all too often find depressingly low down on teachers' lists of priorities).

Of course, this is no longer the most *immediately* fruitful area of cultivation with most children, for whom the television and the cinema provide an instantly accessible form of entertainment; but as long as the *fun* of reading is kept firmly to the fore, near miracles can be performed.

My reservations about school libraries, with their dismayingly large and often confusing stock of books, had hitherto been silenced by the institution of the Library and the library lesson. But when the Raising of the School Leaving Age brought with it its own crisis of shortage of space and our Library had to be used as a full-time classroom for no less than *two* junior Humanities classes, the matter was decided for me and I went ahead full-scale with the decentralisation of reading books into separate class libraries.

Each teacher had a stock of reading books in his or her own room, chosen from the school's own book-stock and from the County Library issue according to the age of the children to be taught in that room. (Matters are made somewhat easier here by our block time-tabling, which means that almost all teachers work with only two, and sometimes one year-group, which cuts down the range of books that are needed in any one room.) As a matter of policy, I chose only those County Library hardbacks which were immediately attractive to look at and which would appeal to the predominantly working class children at the school. Jennings, for example, is *not* well received! For the books that I bought, I chose paperbacks virtually throughout. These, although they obviously do not last as long as hardbacks, are more attractive, and because they are thinner, are psychologically a better buy. The ability range was covered by the Aub 75 and Topliner series for the lower end through Puffins and Peacocks up to ordinary Penguin and Pan books for fifth years. My own attitude is that it is better for a child to read almost *any* book than no book at all, and that the old methods of "stimulating" reading, such as insisting on an essay on every book read or setting a test at the end of the year on a previously prescribed list of classics, are virtually guaranteed to have the opposite effect in the mixed ability situation.

Nonetheless, stimulation *is* necessary, and I have found the intimacy of the classroom libraries very useful in this respect. Not only can the teacher choose a book from the shelf and by careful selection ensure that at least some (usually the majority!) of the class will want to read it, but he can help children with their individual choices because he above all will know their tastes and aptitudes in reading. The problem of children reading books above or below their own standard is nowhere near as serious as some would like to make out; the less able will swiftly regulate themselves to a book they can cope with and will be inclined to aim for more difficult and demanding ones, provided the teacher encourages informal feedback among the children as to what the books are like and what tastes they would suit. I never forbid a more able child to read a simple reader, and indeed I think that it is no bad thing for them to whizz through a book well below their standard within an hour. I have never found that they are permanently loathe to read to their own standard, and, after a short time, the slightest hint is enough to get them back to their own level.

Similarly, I give classes the option of bringing in their own books or those they have borrowed from the library to read in the class-reading lessons (which I set aside as a regular session in the Lower forms, but which I leave on a more informal footing in the fourth and fifth years.) I openly encourage reading as an alternative if a child is uninterested in, or bored by, a piece of work, and find that this alternative is rarely abused.

The individual teacher will have to decide for himself whether or not he is willing to accept (i) Alistair Maclean, (ii) James Bond, (iii) Enid Blyton, (iv) Jackie or (v) The Beano (presumably in that order!) as permissible reading in class. I have found no hard-and-fast rule that is useful in those circumstances and suggest that most restrictions on choice in this field run the risk of being counter-productive. Nonetheless, each individual must have his own standards if he is to be respected as a teacher and educator, and the children will usually accept a reasonable demarcation line between what is and what is not acceptable, if it can be honestly and reasonably justified. I see the main danger in the teacher who has been so affected by the conventional "this-is-good - this-is-bad" syndrome that he becomes blinded both to the needs of his pupils, and, still more seriously, to the wealth of finely written fiction that is on the market at the moment.

More spectacularly, replete with light shows, exciting corners, quizzes and competitions, our School Book Fair seemed to go some way toward making up for the total lack of any form of bookshop in the area. Every child in the school visited the Fair once during lesson time during its week's run, and they were invited to browse, buy or order books either then or at break or lunchtime. Extra staff often had to be called in to cope with the hoards! Parents were also invited to attend, on the theory that, if they were impressed enough to shell out 20p or so, their children might follow suit. Reading as a pastime with a readily available selection of books in the home, is often taken for granted with brighter children but all too easily written off in non-grammar schools. By stressing the enjoyment angle of reading we surprised even ourselves with the enthusiasm for books that the children showed.

The Book Fair itself was backed up by the encouragement of individual class tutors, and its impetus has been capitalised upon by the setting up of a School Bookshop by one of the members of staff concerned. This retails a fairly wide, varied selection of fiction and non-fiction, all at reasonable prices, and at varying standards of difficulty. This has both advantages and disadvantages, since like the Library it can all too easily become a daunting, impersonal institution; but staffed by a sympathetic and imaginative teacher, and backed by the support of other English teachers in the school, it can serve a useful purpose, especially when there is no other bookshop readily available.

Another alternative (or possible back-up) to the Bookshop are such clubs as the Scoop Book Club, run by Scholastic Publications, which retail a wide range of attractive and reasonably priced books and issue in advance of them eye-catching publicity material and helpful hints for the teacher on the possible chronological and reading age they might suit. The principal advantage of the *class* Book Club, as with the class library, is that the teacher can more intimately guide the unsure, even antagonistic pupil.

Above all, a child's individual choice of book will enable him or her to read what he likes *at his own speed,* and indeed anyone who thinks he can class-teach mixed ability classes àll the time, so that every child present is at the same stage of learning is fooling himself. The initial stimulus can be and often will be the same for all the children, but after that each individual must be allowed to proceed at a pace suitable to his own ability.

Nowhere is this more true than with creative writing where the traditional approach -
Teacher: *"Write me an essay entitled 'The Lost Treasure'".*
Bright Pupil: *"How long, sir?"*
Teacher: *"Minimum of three sides."*
- is a dead duck. That is the easiest way I know to ensure that you get the worst from virtually all your pupils. The wily intelligent child will restrict his thinking to the prescribed limit and to not a jot further, and the less able, unable to meet the specified limit, will either drop out of the race or produce three sides of demoralised scrawl, in which no creative energy is in evidence after the first half-side. The demands, like the work must be tailored to the individual needs of the child, which means that virtually every child will need to be advised personally on what every piece of work means to him. This need not be as onerous for the teacher as it sounds, since the

children can quickly be advised of the standard expected for them personally, and will proceed from that point.

Similarly, it is worse than useless to have a system of assessment that repeatedly places the most able children at the "top" of the class, and the least able at the "bottom". This is so destructive in almost all its ramifications that I am surprised that it has lasted as long as it has in our Grammar schools and, alas, in some of our less enlightened Comprehensives and Secondary Modern schools. The only system that will work with mixed ability groupings is one which takes into account on the one hand the *effort* a child has made, regardless of his inherent ability (thus making "A's" not only possible but also desirable for those in the lower reaches of literacy and oracy), and also their *attainment* within the bounds of their abilities. It is only in the final stages of the fifth year that a more absolute system of attainment is necessary for external purposes.

However, when much of the time is spent with children working at their own speed, possibly on different assignments, it is useful for the teacher to have one tool with which to establish himself for at least part of the time as being firmly and visibly in control; a time to unify and draw together the job in hand. Here the class set-book, so much reviled in recent years, fulfills a useful purpose, since a sensitively chosen novel, read well to the whole class, will offer them a shared experience from which they can draw at their different levels of ability, whilst *enjoying* the reading almost as one.

I do stress, however, that the book must be read well - if necessary by the teacher throughout. I will give any child the option of reading initially, and will encourage the really excellent reader to read a page or two to give me a "breather", but, for the most part, the teacher is the best equipped to instil life and interest into a book and to make the most of what it has to offer, if only because he alone has read the book beforehand.

The problem of those children who reach Secondary age without being able to read must be faced, and faced squarely, if a school is not going to build up a backlog of problems for itself in the final year, when the now disgruntled adolescents, realizing that school has failed to provide them with a suitable education for the past ten or eleven years, will see no reason why they should continue to co-operate on its terms, and begin to make their (inevitably unacceptable) own. The remedial child can and should spend a great deal of his time with his own form group, and, until the beginning of tailor-made ROSLA courses at fourteen to fifteen, will benefit extensively from this, socially if not always academically, (as will the brightest children, since that, too, is what mixed ability teaching is about). However, for a certain time, *daily* - for progress will be inhibited if each day does not take up from the one before - such children need assistance in reading and basic Mathematics such as cannot be given by the non-specialist in the full-class situation. At Northcliffe we have a Reading Centre, which is furnished with highly specialised equipment - and carpets and armchairs. Such an attractive and comfortable room acts as an incentive for the children to be relaxed and responsive and makes it less likely that they will be resentful of going there. It is staffed by a full-time remedial teacher, who not only organises the children but also advises other staff on the content and style of their courses. Indeed, such a teacher might well develop in time into a full-time adviser and programme designer, and the actual remedial work might come to be done exclusively by the regular teacher in normal class time, perhaps with occasional tutorials with the remedial specialist.

As yet, however, we have to content ourselves with a system of extraction from ordinary lessons, which must be worked out care-fully if it is not to be counter-productive - for instance extracting children from Mathematics to do reading! Similarly, care must be taken not to extract children from lessons they enjoy or may benefit from in other ways, such as Art and Craft or Cookery or Needlework.

This might seem to be something of a sell-out to any extreme mixed ability idealist, and to a point perhaps it is; but I am a firm believer in not throwing out the baby with the bath water and have learnt from experience that certain hoped-for situations never arise in the mixed ability class. These are almost exclusively on the academic (rather than the social) side. I have never, for example, seen a very able child go and help one considerably less able than himself, unless asked to do so. This is not to say that the mixing of abilities has failed here, simply that its benefits enable children of different abilities to accept and understand each other's differences without necessarily being willing or able to do anything about them. And surely no-one would advocate a return to the old pupil-teacher situation. Similarly, I have rarely seen those finding extreme difficulty with their work being impelled toward success by the sight of those brighter than themselves achieving it. They will accept it - but accept it as inevitable and part of the natural way of things.

In fact, unavoidable difficulties can arise at the fifteen to sixteen stage in the run-up to examinations. This year I have taught, to a single mixed ability class, a common CSE, GCE "O" level syllabus in the Humanities, which in theory provides for those below CSE as well as for the two examination levels. Yet I found it difficult to maintain an overall balance between the needs of those whose work was to be submitted for "O" level (and who perforce needed to be somewhat pressurised) and those who could be allowed to work at their own speed as usual. The former, in this case, were occasionally rather peeved about the latter - an irrational attitude perhaps, but nonetheless an understandable one. Again, a compromise was reached, when a colleague and myself, having adjacent classrooms, gave the children the option of working in one room where they could work at their own pace and talk when they wanted, or the other where they would have to work in silence and under pressure. Ability was ignored, and inclination to work was the sole criterion of choice. Surprisingly two thirds chose to be quiet, and all were happy with the ensuing situation - students and teachers!

My predecessor as Head of English at Northcliffe once said to me: *"There are two things that every child, no matter what his ability, can do - one is to write verse, the other is to act."*

For my own part, I have slight reservations about the verse writing, since, although I would agree that it is possible to develop an awareness of poetry and even the ability to write it in almost any child, in many cases it is all too unnatural and strained a medium to offer means of genuine, unaffected expression to many children. I have never found this the case with drama, however.

In using the term "drama", a definition is perhaps necessary. I am not referring to the largely discredited process of reading one act plays around the class - largely discredited, but unfortunately all too common, even today. Nor do I necessarily mean those highly demanding and ultimately rewarding schemes of dance/drama, which have found such success (usually when taught by qualified teachers) in many Secondary schools. Nor finally do I lay particular stress on such abstract forms as mime, which like poetry will often alienate at least a section of a class. Instead I refer to what I would loosely call "improvisation" - be it on a theme, of a set passage, through role-play or whatever - which, without a doubt, I have found to build more bridges between mixed ability groups than any other form of teaching I have encountered.

Here, as elsewhere, the teacher should have his own standards and expectations, and it is far from desirable for the teacher to accept without question what is produced first time round since, in the initial stages at least, all that he will get is "types" culled from magazines and comics and watered down versions of what was seen on the television the night before. However, it does not take long to get past that stage to where one can draw on first-hand ideas and real experience - in which the so-called ability of the child (that is the ability to read and write) is irrelevant. Indeed, within the past few weeks I was astonished to discover that the reason why one of the most talented and sensitive children in my evening drama club had missed a session was that he had been attending an extra session at the Reading Centre at that time. Yet here was a boy, whom I had only known through the medium of drama and whom I had marked as one of the most sensitive and able children in the group, but who, on conventional grading, would come at the bottom of his class in English! One might well wonder, this being so, why drama is not used more frequently, more integrally by every English teacher.

Of course, the old arguments against drama are much repeated. The children are inhibited and derivative in what they do. But so are they in any subject unless they are given guidance and help in the initial stages at least. Difficulties about noise and control are also stressed - but again, a good teacher will have no more difficulty in controlling a drama lesson than any other; possibly less, since almost all children enjoy doing drama. All too often, even in more enlightened schools, I feel that these are just the rationalisations of teachers who are either unsure how to handle a drama lesson or who feel guilty if the children are not reading, writing or "discussing".

Yet, above all, it is in the floating up of ideas that drama scores. Many children who would be incapable of formulating an abstract concept, or even an example of it in concrete form, can do just that - because others can *see* as well as hear what he means. Drama can often be followed by a discussion of the points that were raised in the improvisation, seemingly centred upon the "technique" of the drama but effectively examining the insights revealed.

And what of school productions and the theatre? I personally maintain that there is a place for the former, not so much for the inherent quality of the drama they contain but because the tension and excitement that the element of public performance generates can provide a satisfying climax to a term or year and a memorable experience which, it would seem, can last long after the child has left the school. The school play can also offer a vehicle for the child who in most other respects has little opportunity to stand out from the throng, to be an important segment of a whole - a vital cog in the wheel. Nor need the longest parts necessarily be given to the best readers, with the willing but less able pupils as spear carriers. In spite of initial sight reading difficulties, I have seen children of well below average academic ability grow visibly in stature during rehearsals to overtake their erstwhile superiors on the home straight, once the barrier of learning the words has been overcome.

The same can be said of trips to the theatre. In what was one of the five original Educational Priority Areas, there is obviously little history of theatre or concert going. Yet I have seen grow, initially through the energies of the teachers who organised the trips but soon of its own volition, a group of discerning theatregoers, who in the last year have attended The Royal Ballet, two plays at Stratford-upon-Avon almost half the productions at the Crucible Theatre in Sheffield, to say nothing of several pop concerts! Nor has the group drawn its members from those sections of the school who might naturally be expected to be theatre fodder. The school's policy of organising trips to all types of entertainment, high-brow and low, has meant that children who enjoyed the trip to see Slade or The Strawbs, have been willing to give a weekend at Stratford a try, whereas their first reaction would normally have been *"Get lost!"* By laying the stress on the actual event rather than on what is to be seen, it has proved possible to attract a far wider range of children; and for all that this means in insults to the Bard among others - that the trip was advertised as "A Weekend in Stratford, plus a visit to Coventry Cathedral (and see two plays at the Theatre)" - the number of those who went, enjoyed themselves *and* wanted to go again more than justified the heresy.

In conclusion, I would say that a teacher must be something of a showman to be a success in a mixed ability situation. We have all seen the stony inevitability that poor, unexciting teaching produces in Secondary Modern schools, where children show their disapproval with their feet and stay away, or sit passive like lambs to the (preferable?) slaughter. Equally, we all know the travesty of education that sometimes takes place in places where the children are intelligent enough to realize that the desired examination passes are to be had by drawing from the knowledge of the teacher, but not militant enough to insist that he makes his knowledge more palatable, more interesting. But with a mixed ability class a certain, almost intangible dynamic exists, which prevents the teacher from churning out the same old turgid stuff and forces him to present his wares in a more exciting way, if they are to be acceptable to those he is being paid to teach.

Whether this dynamic comes from the less able and spurs on the brighter children to more open discontent; or whether it emanates from the high-flyers and finds its expression in the more average I cannot exactly say. But exist it does, and it is perhaps this spur to better teaching that makes mixed ability groupings so desirable, indeed essential in these changing and difficult times.

Chapter 9
Social Studies

S.K. Legon

I have been teaching children in mixed ability groups for so long that being asked to describe how one does it is like being asked how you drive a car when the whole process is automatic, although you adjust all the time to the hazards and prevailing conditions.

At my school we were not suddenly presented with the conversion of the whole school to mixed ability groups; it was gradually introduced starting with the first year forms, who spent a large part of the week learning through interdisciplinary enquiry. I welcomed the opportunity to enter into one-to-one and small group relationships with the pupils. As a result of working in a team with other teachers I learned a great deal about the ways in which knowledge could be sought through experience and presented in a variety of forms. Having had a highly academic formal education myself, removed from the creative area of the timetable at fourteen, it was a revelation to me to see the exploration of ideas and emotions through the visual Arts, Music and Art of Movement.

Interdisciplinary enquiry called for the ability on the teacher's part to organise individual pupil's courses of study, as well as forming groups to explore areas of common interest, and to provide them with the relevant resources and trust them to work without constant overt supervision. It was from watching the pitfalls of this system, and also the benefits, that I realised that if the study of Sociology was to be meaningful to them, then I must approach the teaching of my subject through experimental techniques.

I had started teaching Sociology in a rather orthodox way and achieved a small measure of success with the brighter children. Each lesson, however, developed into a mere dialogue between them and me which was highly enjoyable for us but the others were left far behind, and eventually I realised that this was far from satisfactory and most unfair to the less able child.

My breakthrough came when I was given third forms to teach in a curriculum that had now developed from a very flexible form to one which still gave scope for flexible teaching methods but had a more secure structure both for teachers and pupils. Knowing the nature of third years, as do we all in the profession, I determined to demonstrate methods of social control in the classroom and not just talk about them in the academic sense.

Imagine the scene as twenty-five girls rush into a room, ready to dive into chairs in their favourite parts of the room, sitting next to their friends as is their time-honoured custom. Then the unimaginable happened: they were confronted by a loud-voiced, authoritative and very determined teacher who had hitherto been seen as a kind, lenient, easy-going person, ordering them outside the room, and actually insisting that they line up in silence, and be counted in groups of her choosing to sit where she directed. Inwardly I expected a nasty rebellion, but everyone by now was so mystified that they went in like lambs. In the total silence that followed, I handed out a piece of paper for each group with the sharp command to leave it there until further orders were given. Then I held up a brick and asked them as a group to write down as many uses for it as they could think of in ten minutes, stating that this was a competition. To my amazement everyone actually carried out their task. Each group went to work, keeping their voices down so that the other group would not eavesdrop. After the ten minutes were up, I read out the lists and announced the winners. I then asked them to write down, in a set style, like an experiment in science, what took place in the group. I said they could collaborate on the reports and discuss it among themselves in case some people had poor recall or had difficulty in spelling.

I repeated this process for six more lessons, making the task more difficult as time went on. Having prided myself on being a progressive and liberal teacher up to now, I blushed with shame one day when our chief "villain" of that time announced that she liked this lesson because *"Mrs. Legon makes you behave"*. Later on we were able to discuss this statement and consider its significance to the whole concept of social control.

During this course of group dynamics, I kept changing the size and composition of the group, so that they were forced to work with people they did not know very well, although they had been in the same class for two years. One very shy, withdrawn girl told me later that as a result of this experience she had summoned up the confidence to join a Youth Club, since she had to stop relying on her one friend, also shy, for company.

At one stage the Humanities teachers combined to focus on four specific conditions of human life: oppression, doom, happiness and, in my case, frustration. My group thought they were going to work on frustrating the other groups, but anger overtook them in the end when they realised that I had so engineered events that, as it turned out, they were the ones who suffered the frustration. They were shown how easy it is to mislead groups of people by promises, apparent co-operation, seeming support from a respected leader. This was a somewhat hazardous enterprise from my point of view, but later on, when their intense reactions had cooled, they came to realise the significance of the whole operation from the sociological point of view.

I noticed that this course had benefited the less able pupils considerably. When asked to write their reports, they were able to do so, firstly because the experience was so fresh in their minds and closely connected with them personally, and, secondly, because they could draw on help from the others since I had expressly stipulated that this was desirable.

As usual in Social Studies lessons, discussion plays a major role and is very popular. We do not set out deliberately to promote a discussion but prefer to let one develop as the lesson goes on. At first it is a dialogue between the teacher and a pupil who has a question or a point of view, but later more people join in. This is where one has to be sensitive to the needs of several kinds of pupil. Both able and less able may be too shy or put off by the possible reactions of the more dominant members of the group. The slow pupils, too, become bewildered by what they think is a complete change of subject, whereas the quicker-thinking pupils see a development taking place relevant to the starting point of the discussion. I usually stop the flow and beg for a "résumé" of what has been said, to "clarify my mind". When we have retraced our steps, with the addition of a flow diagram on the board, I ask them to write down a brief outline of the course of the discussion. As a result of this, the discussion may be rescued from becoming irrelevant anecdotes or what seems to be a cosy chat, a pleasant way to pass the time spiced with a good laugh now and then. I remember the time when one set of fourth years were given an essay to write: they exclaimed in consternation,

"But what do we write about?"

"What we've been working on during the last three weeks, of course."

"But we were just talking!"

That taught me a lesson, and now I always inform them that what we are discussing and doing now is going to be expressed in written form at a later date. During discussions I make a point of catching the attention of the slower ones and communicating with them silently: a querying look (do you understand/agree/are you all right?), or I raise my eyebrows incredulously at them (doesn't she go *on*?). If it looks as if they have something to say but are not very articulate I remark that other people like Ann, for example, would like to get a word in, sometime, and invite the contribution, helping out if necessary. It is a struggle sometimes to make them listen patiently to each other and not interrupt or call out derisively, but we do succceed as time goes on.

I have found that, since I started teaching mixed ability groups, I raise my sights and can stretch the pupils' minds more than I ever dared attempt before. I try to see how far I can go before I lose them, and keep checking that everyone understands what I'm talking about. If a considerable number confess that I'm way above their heads and they cannot do the assigned work, I drop it and return to it when they are older. Looking back at the things I say to them, I feel that I've taken a course in "How to Win Friends and Influence People", making such ingratiating remarks as *"I'm going to compliment your intelligence now . . ."* or *"You're such an intelligent bunch, you won't mind attempting this . . . I know it's a bit in advance of your years."* Or I might give them the impression that something is difficult, just to give them all a sense of well-being when they achieve good results.

In the third year it is a good idea to give them plenty of activities to perform in groups. It is in the third year of the Secondary school that the pupils really start flexing their muscles. They are no longer the eager beavers who sought to please teachers in the lower school nor is their interest so easily obtained. This is the time when they are meeting with considerable success outside school in their romantic activities, and a time of intense jealousies and outbreaks of vicious bickering inside the school - usually carried over from incidents that have taken place the preceding night. Formerly, close-knit friendship groups break up and re-form, and passions are easily aroused. Teachers of third year classes need all their powers of patience and endurance to survive and somehow convey some knowledge to pre-occupied minds. Swings of mood, typical of the adolescent period, mean that a successful lesson one week may be followed by a disastrous lesson next week. Conflict at home over the usual issues of staying out late, undesirable companions, laziness and untidiness spill over into the school day, and the poor teacher who cannot duck out of the cross-fire receives all the pent-up resentment. Nearly every teenager thinks she is getting a raw deal from her parents and no one else suffers as much as she does.

During this year I attempt to provide work which will not suffer unduly if the pupils are feeling depressed or upset. I find a study of "Persuasion" goes down well at this time, as it gives plenty of scope for the pupils to study their own techniques of persuasion and obtain some insight into their successes or failures. I usually start off by dividing the class into couples: one is to attempt the persuasion and the other is to resist the effort. When they have decided on their respective roles, they discuss the issue at stake.

Popular choices are mother/daughter arguing about going out or new clothes, friend persuading a friend to "own up", sister begging to borrow sister's clothes for a special occasion, and so on. When they are all ready the class assembles in a circle and each group demonstrates to the others in turn. We then discuss the successes and failures. Some mothers-to-be are going to be rather too easy-going for the health of their purses, and some daughters have effectively shown how they get round their fathers.

Following this we move on to how to persuade people to buy things. We assemble a collection of objects, and volunteers choose what they would like to sell. This is the kind of occasion that brings Deputy Heads running if they are at all nervous about noise penetrating classroom walls. Newcomers to teaching would be well advised to warn members of staff in adjoining rooms beforehand. Some pupils resist the temptation to shout their wares and attempt instead the soft, wheedling approach. I thought I'd chosen the wrong line of business when I sold two dozen watches one day. There was a shocked gasp when I whispered that I'd picked them up cheap and "no questions asked". The deception lasted for about two minutes - *"Teachers wouldn't do that sort of thing"*. I don't wish to be accused of slandering the profession, but we did look at several newspapers to see the kind of people who were convicted of embezzlement and similar offences and the pupils were quite surprised that so-called respectable citizens were capable of earning a dishonest living.

After the market-place episode, we went on to selling ourselves, starting with the "Situations Vacant" columns. Each girl chose a job she liked and wrote a letter of application. They also wrote a "Situations Wanted" advertisement too. I then wrote to each girl inviting her to an interview. Being in school uniform they were unable to dress for the occasion, but they described what they would wear and drew a sketch of the chosen outfit. Sometimes I conducted the interview, but usually with "colleagues". Some applicants had to face a whole board of interviewers for important posts. I had to be careful to interview the nervous, shy girls myself since their class-mates might cause too much embarrassment. Each candidate was asked to wait outside the room while we discussed her application form and decided on the questions to be asked. At the end we discussed the finer points of the exercise and assessed the degree of success achieved by each girl.

This kind of activity is popular since it focuses interest on the most fascinating person these egocentrics know - themselves. They are not so interested in the general affairs of the outside world, unless they have a direct influence on their own lives.

Another area of persuasion we looked at was the world of advertising which they explored with one of my students. Again this produced scope for children of all abilities, since it involved the collection of material from the mass media to fit the categories of selling techniques used by the advertisers. They made their own visual forms of advertisement, some of which were extremely witty, and then went on to work in groups on the TV type commercials. Most of these efforts were awful and received the thumbs-down from their very critical audience, reared on a lifetime's commercial TV watching. I finished this course by readings from "Techniques of Persuasion" and talking about "brain washing" methods used in some totalitarian states. All this work is very relevant to their study of the mass media in the fourth year.

I also find it profitable to talk about the methods of coping with conflict situations in the school itself. "How do you persuade the Head to allow you to stay in at break or lunchtime?" We analyse successes with members of staff, especially with myself, since I am School Librarian and they depend on my goodwill to provide them with books on every subject under the sun for work in other lessons. *"Is it advisable to bang on the door and bawl across the room to me for a book on parasites?"*
"Gawd, no."
"Show me what you think I prefer".
A demonstration follows, with a giggle as an individual who is normally the one who does yell at me after knocking the door down behaves like a paragon of virtue on this occasion.

Another exercise in group co-operation we carried out was to set every group a task to carry out over a few weeks' lessons. Examples of work done included making oven gloves, writing pop magazines, preparing a talk on a set subject, completing a large jig-saw puzzle and two groups had to prepare a Call My Bluff game to play against each other. A group recorder was appointed to write a weekly account of the group's progress, noting difficulties and the division of work done, which was of an excellent standard, although we do not really fancy putting the oven gloves to the test. Everyone seemed to enjoy this work and it appealed to all the ability range.

Having spent their first three years in laying the foundations for the Sociology course through a practical approach, we proceed to work of a more formal nature in the fourth year with those pupils who have chosen Elementary Sociology as one of their CSE options in the Humanities. We have adopted the Mode 3 type of examination for the CSE in this subject on a continuous assessment basis, with no final written paper. The course is divided into four parts.

1 In the first two terms of the fourth year we cover the main subject matter. Every three weeks or so, the pupils have to write an essay expressing the knowledge they have gained on the subject they have been studying. I am very conscious of the fact that many of them will be going on to a College of Further Education where they will be required to write in more formal terms, so I spend some time teaching them how to gather relevant material and put it together in a cogent form. At first I thought I would have problems in this respect with the less able children, but I found that they coped very well on the whole. The more able pupils tend to worry more and see complications where none exist. The slower pupils tend to listen carefully, stick closely to their notes and do not venture outside the limit of the subject matter, whereas the brighter pupils, who are usually very articulate and voluble in discussion lessons, run on too much and try to pack everything in. They, in fact, need far more discipline than slower colleagues, since they have this urge to interpret and embroider a theme over much. They also suffer from feelings of frustration more, since they are not completely satisfied with their efforts. Some will try to avoid writing essays for various reasons - *"I can't do this sort of work in school - can I do it at home?"* - or they find it a waste of time sitting in silence for an hour when they could be dazzling the others and me with their intellects. I am quite adamant, however, and sit there until they do. After this initial period of adjustment, they all settle into this routine of three weeks' work followed by the appropriate essay. I also encourage them to illustrate their written work with relevant pictures and articles from newspapers and magazines, and to take photographs

where possible. Additional material can be incorporated later on in the fifth year as well. The essays may be rewritten too if they and I are not satisfied. I offer more encouragement to the less able pupils because it can be rather a strain on them, but when talking to the class as a whole I treat everyone the same. I can soon see from their work and behaviour if anything is too difficult for them to understand, but in the fourth year I press on regardless since I allow time in the fifth year for individual tuition for those pupils who have been absent or have not grasped some essential points.

2 In the third term of the fourth year we embark on the Group Dynamics part of the syllabus, following on course work on the nature of groups. For six periods of an hour each I divide the class into small groups on an arbitrary basis, and these groups change from week to week. A task is set them to carry out, and I vary the environmental conditions as much as I can. At the end of each experiment they write detailed notes on what happened in the group they were in - who took the initiative, who did very little, who contributed most, did they enjoy the task and so on. At the end of these six lessons we discuss fully the implications of the experience, and an essay on the factors that influence group behaviour is written. Since I give them some pretty daft things to do, it always amazes me that they actually participate seriously. It must have something to do with my authoritarian personality. We also teach them, in conjunction with the Maths department, how to carry out social surveys.

3 This is followed in the first term of the fifth year by the Group Research project which forms the third part of the examination. Here they carry out some original research in small groups of their own choosing. Each person has to keep a personal diary of the course of the research, and at the end write an assessment of the contributions made to this research by each member of the group. I myself keep a record of each group's progress and compare it with their accounts. They may go outside the school or the classroom, or stay put, according to their needs. They do not get any help from me and this they find rather frustrating at times: as one girl wrote, *"This work taught me the meaning of independence."* The object of this exercise is not the actual research, but the method used and the use made of their knowledge of group behaviour.

4 The last part of the examination consists of a special study done by

each individual on a subject that interests them most. Many of our
pupils take part in the School's Community Service Scheme, and this
is an ideal opportunity for them to base their study on personal
experience. The girls who are interested in Education work in the
local Primary schools for one morning a week for a term. Those who
are concerned for handicapped children and old people are attached
to the appropriate organisation in the community. Some pupils are
highly obsessed with their own problems and I suggest a study of a
personal nature. One girl recently was involved with a boyfriend who
was a drug-addict, and was relieved to be able to write it all out of
her system together with an objective description of addiction.

Although all this work is within the compass of children of all
abilities, it is in the public examination section that differences of
intelligence and background and all the other factors that influence
a child's progress do show up. The brighter pupils seem to have a
firm grasp of organisation: they understand fully the nature of their
commitments, they keep their material all together in one place, they
have an overall remembrance of the task in hand. The less able child,
on the whole - and there are exceptions of course - tends to panic,
loses sight of her objectives, and literally loses sight of her material or
forgets to bring it to school. They lose interest, too, unless you, the
teacher, are very watchful. Some pupils who dislike school and would
have left early in former times, take themselves off, ostensibly to
carry out research, but in fact to loaf about the neighbourhood. We
feel we must give them freedom and responsiblity in the fifth form,
but a very careful organisation of schedules is needed to avoid the
backsliding to which some children are prone at this age.

Although the future is important to them and they recognise that
qualifications are necessary in a competitive society, our senior
pupils are beset with personal problems which we, as adults, know
are of a transitory nature, but which do have an adverse effect on
their work. The able pupil has the intelligence to place her problems
in proper perspective or may have the ability to put them aside
during school hours; good powers of concentration help a great deal
in this respect. I was talking to a group of Grammar school pupils
recently about this aspect of their lives. I spend every day of my
school life listening to pupils' worries, as do my colleagues, and we
are not surprised at what we hear, but when I described the kinds of
difficulties our senior pupils encounter to this group of girls they

reacted with surprise. They seemed not to be subject to the worries that our pupils have - parents' matrimonial problems, conflict between daughter and parent, romantic setbacks, depression, a sense of worthlessness, mentally handicapped siblings, being in love - just to mention a few. Either these girls live in convent-like seclusion, have happy families and perfect conditions for home study, or they are blessed with an intelligence that enables them to cope, or are so single-minded academically that they are less affected by their emotional states. I must confess to not knowing which of these is the case.

In conclusion, I feel that the term "mixed ability" is a red-herring thrown across the path of would-be teachers to frighten them, I should imagine. There is no such thing as a mixed ability group, but there again, there is! The top stream of a Grammar school contains children who have different strengths and weaknesses as does the bottom stream of a Secondary Modern. Even where subjects are taught in sets, like Mathematics and Languages, there is still a range of performance, as can be seen from the examination results at the end of term. Although I do not make a practice of this, I have taken a close look at one year group of this school and tried to sort them into four "ability" groups. The resulting lists showed a small bottom and top group, and enormous classes in between whom I could not accommodate comfortably in my room. I prefer to have the talents and weaknesses spread evenly throughout the classes, and then I get some lovely surprises when some of the so-called less able pupils outclass the intellectuals.

Professor Eysenck has suggested that it is personality we should be considering and not just the IQ score of our pupils. Once again the thoughts of mere teachers, who realised this long ago, hit the head-lines when they come out of the mouths of experts. We are making it a habit now in our Social Studies department of arranging our examination groups on the basis of personality factors. When we receive the lists of the girls who have chosen to take Social Studies for CSE in their fourth and fifth years, we first of all decide who "clang and chime" with each one of us, then we work out which villain should be parted from her fellow villain and which pupils would feel more secure with people they know well. We leave until last, the question of ability, but we assess that in "contributive/non-contributive" terms. We prefer a balance in each group, so that we don't have one group of acutely shy, tongue-tied girls, or another group of highly eloquent strident young ladies. When one analyses the examination results at the end of the course there are few surprises: the bright ones achieve high grades and most of the less able pupils score lower grades, but there are usually some outstanding feats of performance from those pupils who have become so stimulated and involved in their work that they could not help doing well. Continuous assessment helps these children, and they are glad to have the strain of a written examination removed from their path. I would hope that by the end of the course most of them have arrived at some degree of self-awareness and have been set thinking about the social needs and problems of people for a lifetime. Although I am as much interested in achieving good results in public examinations as anyone else, I am far more concerned about the development of social relationships.

I cannot affirm confidently that the way I teach Social Studies to mixed ability groups is one hundred per cent successful since conditions change from year to year, but one does grow increasingly aware of one's difficulties as a teacher as time goes on, and it is necessary and vital to go on working at better ways of organizing courses to meet the needs of the whole ability range.

Chapter 10
Mathematics

P.A. Prettyman

Crown Woods is a large co-educational London Comprehensive school. It suffers at the moment from many of the problems common to most London schools: a difficulty in obtaining and retaining experienced staff; an overused and inadequate building. However at Crown Woods none of these problems has (yet) reached an impossible level. Furthermore it has many distinct advantages enjoyed by few London Comprehensives. The building is, after all, purpose built; the staff, though mostly young, is enthusiastic and well qualified; and the intake of children covers the full social and educational spectrum. It is this last factor which makes the Crown Woods experience in teaching children as mixed ability groups particularly interesting. The Primary school gradings of my own first year tutor group illustrate most clearly this range of intake - there are seven band ones, fifteen band twos and eight band threes. There are a couple of children who are notably academic with a high level of written expression and three who, when they arrived, were total non-readers.

Crown Woods, because if its size - 2,200 at the last count - is organised largely on a "house" basis and the children's basic unit is the house orientated tutor-group. Each group contains about thirty children who have been selected to form as near a balanced mixed ability group as possible; the selection is done by examination of primary profiles and interviews with children and parents.

The mixed tutor group has been a feature of the school since it started in 1958, but it is only in recent years that it has existed for other than registration and pastoral purposes. Two years ago for a whole series of reasons streaming and setting were abolished for the first year and the children started to have all their lessons together. Largely in the light of the success of the first year, each separate subject department decided whether it wanted to continue to teach in the same way in the second year. All, with the exception of the Modern Languages Department, decided to do so. A similar choice is now being made for the third year: this time Physics, Chemistry and Geography (two lessons of each) are also setted, but the main bulk of the teaching in the third year will continue to be in mixed ability groups.

I have outlined only the basic structure of the school as it now is. My main aim in this contribution is to describe the development of mixed ability teaching within the Mathematics Department. It must be said that each subject department has (for good or evil) developed its own method of organising its courses best suited to its own individual needs, aims and philosophy, and any arguments and objectives outlined below are only those that have been thrashed out within the Mathematics Department. Since the Department is eighteen-strong, arguments have been well thrashed.

The full reasons why the Mathematics Department was in the forefront of the push, two years ago, for a full mixed ability first year are fairly complex. Suffice it to say that there were both external and internal reasons. Amongst the external ones was the ILEA's decision to cut the Primary school leaving grades from seven to three, and one of the most significant of the internal reasons was the presence of a young and enthusiastic group within the department, who believed completed in the "rightness" of teaching in mixed ability groups and who were prepared to carry out all the necessary research and writing to get the scheme off the ground.

One of the arguments against mixed ability which confronted us was that, of all the subjects which are taught in schools, Mathematics would be the most difficult to teach without streaming the children.

At Crown Woods we believe we have shown this argument to be completely fallacious and that in fact the structure of the subject can be used to help the process of learning - by breaking the structure down into basic concepts and building it up in the child's mind by a series of small but definite steps, like building bricks or in a flow diagram. Obviously the nature of Mathematics, like all disciplines, is more subtle and complex than this rather simplistic outline tends to suggest. A developed mathematician is aware that there exist relationships between the simplest basic concepts and the furthest boundaries of the subject, and it is the teacher's job to highlight such inter-relationships when they arise. Nevertheless, the fact that structure stands out more clearly in Mathematics assists the teacher in finding a gradual but systematic process of learning.

The material

After much discussion it was decided to arrange the first year content into fifteen or so topics, each containing one or two basic concepts, and to write a set of work-cards on each topic. Topics chosen covered a wide range such as Plotting Points, Symmetry, Statistics, Fractions, Angles, Mappings and Relationships, but were largely chosen so as to present a good selection of new ideas and concepts to children without arousing any fears and inhibitions from their Primary schools.

Each topic is presented as a set of work cards. The number of cards in each set varies considerably but the usual number is eight or nine. In all cases the aim of a set of cards is to present the conceptual idea or principle in as simple a form as possible within the first two or three cards. On these cards the language and style are as simple and straightforward as the topic allows. The succeeding cards then practise and develop the idea or technique at a level with which the majority of children can cope. The set is then completed by a couple of cards in which the topic is given a bit of depth with the style and language correspondingly more complex.

Clearly the effectiveness of this approach depends very much on the way this material is actually used, and, as I hope to show later, there is a range of different ways in which this work can be used in the classroom.

This then is the pattern on which we have tried to model all our first year work. To illustrate this, here is an example of one of the topics. Entitled "POINTS" it has the objective of teaching children that any point on a plane can be determined by an ordered pair - Cartesian co-ordinates.

Points
Fixing Points

A

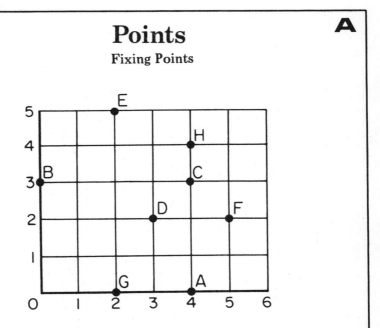

A number line has been drawn across the page and from the same starting point O another number line has been drawn up the page. Where is the dot marked C?

To get to C from the starting point go *along* 4 and then *up* 3.

C is the point (4,3)

Notice that the *first* number in the bracket is the *along* number and the *second* number is the *up* number.

(4,3) is called an *ordered pair.*

Write down in your book the pairs of numbers which fix the positions of A,B,C,D,E,F,G,H.

This card establishes the concept. It explains as simply as we have been able to make it that a point on a grid is fixed by a pair of numbers.

A few children may need some verbal support, but only those whose reading is weak, and the rest of the class grasp the idea very easily. Some teachers prefer to replace card A by a classroom discussion which can have the effect of stimulating the interest of the children more effectively.

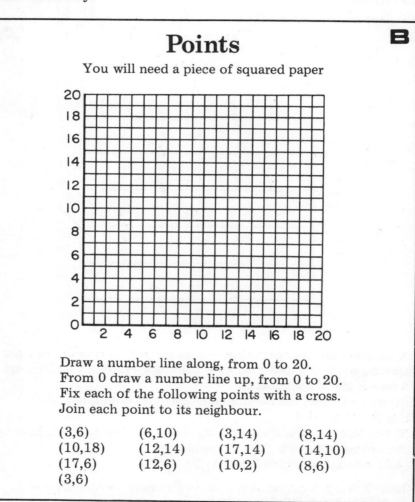

Points B

You will need a piece of squared paper

Draw a number line along, from 0 to 20.
From 0 draw a number line up, from 0 to 20.
Fix each of the following points with a cross.
Join each point to its neighbour.

(3,6)	(6,10)	(3,14)	(8,14)
(10,18)	(12,14)	(17,14)	(14,10)
(17,6)	(12,6)	(10,2)	(8,6)
(3,6)			

This is the first of several cards which get the children to draw a shape by joining dots up in an order. A simple symmetrical shape like this is good for a start since it assists the children to plot the points correctly.

A later card which exploits the same idea is card H.

Points **H**

Use Squared Paper

Draw a number line from 0 to 28 along.
Draw a number line from 0 to 28 up.
Plot the following groups of points.
In each group, join each point to its neighbour.

Group 1

(8,13)	(7,12)	(8,11)	(9,11)	(12,16)
(11,18)	(7,17)	(6,17)		

Group 2

(18,12)	(18,9)	(20,6)	(23,4)	(23,2)
(22,1)	(25,1)	(25,5)	(24,6)	(25,7)
(26,10)	(27,7)	(27,11)	(25,16)	(18,19)
(9,18)	(6,19)	(3,17)	(2,15)	(2,3)
(3,2)	(4,2)	(5,3)	(5,4)	(4,4)
(4,3)	(3,3)	(3,4)	(4,9)	(6,10)
(6,9)	(7,10)	(8,8)	(9,4)	(9,2)
(8,1)	(11,1)	(11,7)	(12,8)	(12,9)
(11,10)				

Group 3

(12,8)	(13,7)	(17,6)	(20,6)

Group 4

(5,14)	(5,15)	(4,15)	(4,14)	(5,14)

This card is highly successful, and although there are four cards of this type in the set, the children very much enjoy using them.

The cards between B and H use battleships, a map, letters of the alphabet, all to reinforce the same idea.

Card J extends the idea of plotting points into plotting straight lines and suggests that there might be a relationship between the coordinates.

Points J

Draw number lines from 0 to 20

1
Plot these points. Join each one to its neighbour:

(1,2) (3,6) (5,10) (7,14) (10,20)

What shape do you get?

Can you see a connection between the along number and the up number for each of the points?

2
Plot the following sets of points. Draw each set on a different piece of squared paper. In each set, join each point to its neighbour.

(a)	(1,1)	(7,7)	(9,9)	(10,10)	(15,15)
(b)	(3,1)	(6,2)	(12,4)	(15,5)	(18,6)
(c)	(1,8)	(4,11)	(6,13)	(8,15)	(10,17)
(d)	(8,3)	(9,4)	(12,7)	(16,11)	(20,15)

Can you find a connection between the along number and the up number for each set?

K again explores another idea that would normally be met at a much higher level.

Points

K

Plot on squared paper the following pairs of points and join up each pair with a straight line.

(a)	(2,4)	and	(2,6)
(b)	(5,3)	and	(1,3)
(c)	(2,9)	and	(6,5)
(d)	(8,0)	and	(0,2)
(e)	(1,2)	and	(5,8)

Write down the positions of the middle point of each of the lines. Example — the middle point of the line (a) is (2,5).

Try to find out a way of knowing the middle point of the line joining (8,3) and (6,5) *without* plotting the points.

Look carefully at the answers you found for (a) to (e).

Clearly, not all the children may complete the whole set of cards but this will not matter so long as the faster children reach the end when the slowest has completed the introduction and is on the practice - the principle has been learned.

As with all our work this set of workcards was hand written out on a spirit master and enough copies for three or four sets run off. At the end of the initial year this, and all the other topics, was re-discussed and edited to produce a better finished final version. This version is written with Letraset and indian ink then electro-scanned to produce a master stencil: this technique, if the master copies are filed, can produce an almost infinite supply of copies (paper supplies permitting!)

For each topic the teacher receives an envelope file containing
a stack of transparent plastic envelopes, each containing thirty-five
copies of one worksheet. Each child also has a transparent plastic
envelope in which he places his current worksheet. This system
protects the worksheets and gives them a reasonable life-span.

A couple more example cards from our first year topics are
reproduced below to give a broader illustration of the approach.

∏umber Bases

A

Take a copy of the sheet called *'DOTS'*.
With a pencil, ring 7 of the dots in a.

Like this

How many dots are left over?

In your books write down first the number of rings,
then the number of dots left over.

Like this

a. 1   2

If there had been more dots
Like this

The answer would have been   2   4

Do this for all the groups of dots on the sheet.

Statistics

A traffic survey was carried out in Eltham High Street. For every vehicle a 1 was marked on paper. 11 means 2 vehicles, ~~1111~~ means 5 vehicles.
~~1111~~ 11 means 7 vehicles. Here are the results:

CAR	~~HHT~~ ~~HHT~~ ~~HHT~~ ~~HHT~~ ~~HHT~~ ~~HHT~~ ~~HHT~~ ~~HHT~~ ~~HHT~~ ~~HHT~~ ~~HHT~~ III
LORRY	~~HHT~~ ~~HHT~~ ~~HHT~~ ~~HHT~~ ~~HHT~~ ~~HHT~~ I
BUS	~~HHT~~ ~~HHT~~ ~~HHT~~ IIII
CYCLE	~~HHT~~ I
MOTOR BIKE	~~HHT~~ ~~HHT~~ III

Show the results on a bar chart

Five candidates stood at a *general election.* Here are their votes.

Fred Smith	7,500
Jo Gordon	10,000
Frank Brown	12,000
Cyril Thompson	3,000
Bert Simpson	4,500

Show the results on a bar chart

Get a page in a book or newspaper. Choose a part with about 200 words in it. Draw a bar chart to show how many one letter words, two letter words, three letter words etc . . . . there are.
What is the most common length word?

The first year is therefore presented as a range of work with fifteen possible starting places, each with fourteen possible routes through the year, but clearly in the second and third year the hierarchical aspect of the subject assumes a more dominant role and although we have continued with the topic approach in the second year, the topics have tended to become somewhat larger and more strictly ordered.

Development of the Material in the Third Year

At the end of the second year we have had to come face to face with an all important problem: the "O" level and CSE examinations. The examination courses at Crown Woods cover two years and unfortunately the two examinations are very different. There is in fact a streamed examination system which is inevitably hampering the development of mixed ability teaching in the senior years of the Secondary school. Until the introduction of the common 16+ examination, this is a problem which unfortunately cannot be avoided. At Crown Woods, the Maths Department has decided to develop a three year unstreamed foundation course which attempts to raise all children to the position where as many as possible can continue on an "O" level course in the fourth and fifth year. We must therefore approach the third year with the understanding that there must be an acceleration of pace and deepening of content, in which the principle of individual pacing will probably not be enough. Consequently we are being particularly careful in the third year to take into account individual ability and attainment level as well as pacing.This will demand a branching pattern for the work. It is clear that we will need to have a thorough and reliable assessment of each individual child before we decide which is the right course for him or her. The third year work is being structured with that in mind and is having assessment built into it.

It was agreed that our course will need to incorporate the following characteristics:-

1 The opportunity for all children to follow the same basic course, but at different levels to allow the free range of ability and attainment.
2 The flexibility to swop children from one level to another (frequently if necessary) in an attempt to find the *maximum* work level of which each child is capable.
3 The necessity of revision of first and second year topics for some children and not for others.
4 The ability to return all children to the same point on the pattern to allow for meaningful class based lessons as well as individually based work.

It is quite likely that such a scheme would not have been possible (if indeed desirable!) when we first introduced mixed ability teaching to the first year. However, it is felt by those in the Department who have been responsible for developing mixed ability work, that there is now the confidence and experience to tackle such a scheme, based along the following lines:-

1 The work in the third year falls naturally into three major topics or "cores":-
    a   Number
    b   Algebra and graphs
    c   Shape
    In each of these a central common progression of ideas can be found that covers the syllabus.
2 Each sub-topic with the central common chain of each "core" should be written at two or three levels: simple, standard, advanced, and can be numbered appropriately. This may mean that a card at one level may be equivalent to two or three at another, but it will be possible to shift a child from one level to another at very many points.
3 Further to the central chain of sub-topics there should be a series of extension sub-topics for the extremes of the group, at both ends. There are many natural extensions at the top end of the ability range - graphical treatment of Pascal or Fibonacci numbers, fractional base power series, and natural logs, all of which extend naturally from the basic course. At the lower end of the ability scale the need is for greater variety of graded examples, possibly diagnostic in assessment.

In both Albegra and Number cores, we have suggested a strong emphasis on graph work, which among previous third year students has tended to be a weakness. It is also a much gentler approach well suited to a mixed ability situation. The extension sub-topics for those children coping more easily with the main course include some more open-ended and investigational work (graphs of number patterns, and less common power series) and the opportunity for individual research (power series in the natural world), as well as some fairly advanced new ideas (an investigation of *e* and base-*e* logs). For the less able, the scheme allows for parts to be omitted so that only the major, basic ideas are covered.

Using Work-Cards
As has been brought home to us on numerous occasions, the real key to success is the skill of the teacher. This, of course, is as true (if not more true) of teaching a mixed ability group as of any other group of children. How then do we use this material?

Over the last two years there have been twelve teachers teaching mixed ability Mathematics classes at Crown Woods and this has led to twelve different styles of using the material: ranging from where five or six groups within the class are each working independently on different topics and relying heavily on the work-cards; to rather formalised class-based lessons where the work-cards are used as supplements to the teacher's boardwork and verbal explanations. I have used a variety of methods depending on a number of factors. When we started, I favoured a group-work approach with my own classes and ran the first five topics simultaneously over one term. This experiment was reasonably successful and was dropped only because of our inability, in that first year, to remain at least five topics ahead in our own preparation. Indeed our range of classroom methods was very much determined, at that time, by not having the whole year's work immediately available and there developed a tendency to base most of our lessons on the class-lesson where the complete class was working on the same topic at the same time. Given a free choice this was not necessarily the way we would have developed our classroom organisation. Nevertheless it taught us a considerable amount about the role of the "class-lesson" in the teaching of mixed ability groups, and as we have become more adept at this style of teaching we have come to the unanimous decision that class-based lessons are one of our most valuable ways of teaching children and to go over totally to a group or individual based work scheme would be to lose many of the benefits of *good* class-teaching - the collective experience of participating in the two-way interchange between teacher and child; the awareness of each child's potential and ability to complete a common task. Good education should, after all, never be a lie or a con-trick.

What is really required is a careful blend of styles and methods where the children never become bored with their work *("Not old work sheets again!")* nor the teacher stuck in the monochromatic groove of a single style, so that he becomes as bored and as unimaginative as the worst "chalk-and-talk" teacher whom he thought he was replacing. It is with this in mind that the Crown Woods Maths Department is developing its material, although of course there is a considerable way to go before we achieve the flexibility that we desire. At the moment we have produced self-explanatory teaching material which caters for children of mixed abilities by individualising the pacing. In mixed groups it is usual for only four or five children to experience basic problems with the work so that our system works reasonably well, but there is plenty of room for improvement. The scheme should develop from the strictly linear to contain loops and jumps that will allow the content to be intensified or thinned out for those children who experience specific problems at particular levels, or for those for whom an unnecessarily large amount of time spent dealing with elementary work will lead to the very boredom and carelessness in Mathematics which we were hoping to eliminate. Furthermore, the very able child, of which we have a handful each year, is at the moment being catered for by the basic course, augmented by books and ideas at the disposal of the teacher, but these children's abilities could be harnessed far more productively than we are doing now, and certainly more productively than we have ever done in the past.

Assessing Children in an unstreamed situation

There should be no difference in assessing a child in an unstreamed situation than in a streamed situation: not, that is, if we are assessing the individual child and his progress rather than that of the class as a whole. Unfortunately assessment has adopted several ossified forms in schools and indeed it tends to be regarded with somewhat totemistic reverence by Secondary schools. Before we begin to assess, we need to know exactly *what* it is that we want to assess, and *why* we want to assess it. This is something that can only be worked out in discussion, but here are some starters:-

1 Knowledge content
2 Application of knowledge
3 Logical thinking
4 Problem solving
5 Problem interpretation
6 Fluency with basic skills
7 Fluency with advanced skills (e.g. algebra)
8 Ability to handle abstractions
9 Interest and enthusiasm
10 Level of self-motivation

Priority and ranking among these must be based on the *reasons* for carrying out the assessment. Again, here are some possibilities:-

1 To find out more about the course that has been created, so as to improve it.
2 To learn more about the children in our groups; their rates of learning, depth of understanding, levels of recall and so on.

3 To use what we learn to improve our teaching.
4 To learn more about assessment and the effect it has on children and teachers.

It is clear that if we are to satisfy all of these demands, then we must adopt a range of assessment procedures. This might include three basic methods:-

1 Syllabus-centred, or "across-the-board" examinations and tests.
2 Child-centred tests (selected questions) and individual-based tasks (projects).
3 Continual assessment which could be something more than just test cards at the end of a topic, a system built into the course which would give a meaningful assessment of the child's progress throughout the year.

It has been too easy in the past to link assessment with a number which in some way crystallized an individual child's intellectual capacity, breadth of knowledge, rate of progress and potential development. What is needed is not a number but a picture over time of a child's development - it is against himself that learning can be measured. Mixed ability teaching highlights the individuality of each child and hence throws assessment into a light where it can appear as a productive force, helping the child to learn faster and more efficiently, rather than as a static filter over a group of children in which predetermined values lie. It may even be hoped that one day self-assessment may become a fourth basic method to be added to the three above — but of course we have a long way to go yet.

Reviewing the Progress so far

In many ways it is difficult to analyse objectively what we have gained and lost by destreaming our classes. Nevertheless several factors stand out quite clearly. None of the teachers, at present involved in the scheme, has any doubts that mixed ability teaching has been a success and is an improvement on teaching streamed classes. We feel that, contrary to many criticisms of mixed ability, we are seeing the overall standard of work and the expectation of the children, particularly the less able, improve noticeably. Further-more, we think we can show that the able child is not, and need not be, at any disadvantage: a well planned and prepared course can increase the amount of contact between the teacher and the individual child, particularly valuable for those at the two ends of the ability range. The bright child, probably more than anyone, needs the stimulus of the teacher; in a class of over thirty bright children he rarely gets it. The less able child usually has problems stemming from a basic lack of confidence in his own ability to grasp the subject - particularly true in Mathematics. We have found that the greatest achievement of mixed ability teaching has been to develop the confidence and enthusiasm of all the children and most notably that of the less able. All children appear to hold their initial enthusiasm for longer than before.

From the teacher's point of view the development of mixed ability classes has had several advantages. An end to the "sink class' and the heartache it brings. The opportunity of teaching all types of children and the variety this brings to the classroom situation. There have been many unlooked for gains: the teacher, for some inexplicable reason, seems to be more committed to his class; he is more conscious of the individual abilities of each child and he tends, with all the material available, to try children on more advanced work than otherwise he might have done.

As far as our own particular scheme is concerned, the level of involvement of our teachers in the writing, development and general organisation of our work has produced a very healthy attitude of criticism and self-analysis. At no time do the members of our department feel over-confident or self-satisfied with our scheme. This has led to a continual search for improvement and further development.

Finally I would like to point out that although I am responsible for writing this article (and any false arguments, sweeping statements and pompous comments are therefore mine), it has been based on three years hard work by members of the Maths Department at Crown Woods. Teamwork is always a major asset for a department and it becomes crucial when one is confronted with a new and stimulating challenge.

Chapter 11
Science

D.J. Haslam

Background

Sir Leo Schultz High School was opened in January 1966 as an eleven to eighteen mixed Comprehensive school on a large new estate on the northern boundary of the City of Kingston upon Hull. Initially the pupils were those choosing to come to the school at eleven or electing to transfer from Secondary Modern schools due to close under the reorganization. These pupils wished to continue their education to the end of the fifth year or longer. The initial intakes of pupils were not academically balanced and it was only in 1968 that a genuine Comprehensive entry was received at the age of eleven. It should be stated clearly, however, that any lack of ability of the first pupils was adequately compensated for by enthusiasm and motivation.

In 1968 the reorganization of education in Hull led to a three-tier system and Sir Leo Schultz High School became a thirteen to eighteen High School taking its pupils from a large number of Middle schools. Although the majority of pupils came from about eight schools, over twenty Middle schools in all acted as feeder schools. This, as will be made clear later, provided very real problems. The six main feeder schools are situated on the North Hull Estate, much of which has been built in the last ten years and provides homes for those moved out of the redevelopment areas near to the docks and the city centre. We, like many schools, suffered somewhat from the effects of large-scale redevelopment and its consequential social problems. Unlike many schools in large cities, however, we had very few immigrants and so minimal problems as far as language difficulty was concerned. This is not to say that all children were literate on entering the school, but more about this in due course.

I was appointed as the first Head of Chemistry from September 1968, there already being a Head of Physics (and Science) and a Head of Biology. A team of about twelve staff and three laboratory assistants were responsible for all the science education of about 1500 pupils from the ages of eleven to nineteen. I specifically include the laboratory assistants here as our whole scheme would have been impossible without them. It should also be mentioned that we had a separate Science block comprising nine laboratories of various sizes and two rooms in the general teaching block which were fitted out with movable tables and fixed side benches supplied with gas, water and electricity.

The Local Authority was generous in its allocation of money to set up the laboratories, and the Headmaster, an Arts specialist no less, was equally aware of the requirements and expense involved in establishing practical Science courses! From the outset it was decided that all pupils should study some science and this philosophy has been maintained throughout. It is true to say that in few Comprehensive schools do all pupils follow balanced Science courses. I maintain, however, that it is totally wrong for a girl to study, say, only Biology and a boy only Physics. This belief is reflected in the courses offered which I shall enumerate later.

Reasons for Mixed Ability Teaching
Having previously taught in a Friends' co-educational boarding school I was quite unfamiliar with teaching the less able pupils and I must confess that I was a little shocked by some of my initial contacts and experiences. Even now I am not sure that we know the best method of teaching Science to all pupils but I am convinced that much of what we have done is far better than the traditional class-teaching which may be successfully pursued in selective schools (these, of course, including Grammar and Secondary Modern schools).

It is no part of this article to argue for or against "streaming" - the arrangement of pupils in fixed groups according to ability, the group remaining constant for all subjects - in a Comprehensive school. Suffice it to say that I believe that this is about the worst form of organization and should be totally condemned. I believe that "setting" - the arrangement of pupils for specific subjects in groups according to abilities in those subjects - can be adequately justified, particularly in later years. We, however maintained mixed ability groups for the first two years for the following reasons:

1 In the early years of secondary education it is vital that a child should enjoy his Science. I believe that the swing away from Science in the sixth form which took place in the 1960s could be attributed to a considerable extent to the boring and irrelevant nature of much of the material taught when compared with that of other subjects. With this in mind, it is important that Science should not be merely the accumulation of a vast number of facts. Experience shows that pupils of all abilities have tremendous enthusiasm at the age of eleven and this should be nurtured and cherished as vital to later success. It therefore follows that there is no need to label children as failures at this early point and thus remove all motivation by placing them in "bottom" sets.

2 With the complete freedom which Headteachers have to devise their own curricula and teaching methods, there comes the tremendous difference in the amounts of Science which pupils from different Junior schools have done. Some Junior schools concentrate entirely on project work with the result that it is possible that a pupil can experience very little science. Should this be a reason for labelling him as less-gifted? Equally, of course, Junior school teachers, possibly rightly, may follow their own interests leading to limited teaching in some branches of Science and a thorough study of others.

3 There is little question that "bottom" sets are, in the minds of most teachers, associated with discipline problems. Whatever the reasons for the problems, by teaching in mixed ability groups these problems can be minimised and we can say that with careful supervision even weak disciplinarians have fewer problems.

Course Material

In the early stages after the school opened most of the staff believed, as many Science teachers still do, that they could teach a "somewhat

diluted Grammar school Science" to mixed ability groups. It soon became obvious that we needed to rethink our methods and even to reject class teaching as a basic technique. I remember being asked in my interview as to my views on mixed ability teaching. Since I knew little about it and certainly had no experience of it at all, my reply indicated that this was an impossibility. Whilst it may be possible to teach English or History in this way it was, I believed totally inapplicable to Science. I was then asked whether I would be willing to try it and not wishing to lose the job I readily agreed. I have never regretted the decision. Not only has it resulted in many stimulating sessions of preparation of materials but I believe the results have certainly justified the effort.

In mixed ability teaching the general aim is to get the best out of each pupil. He should perform no less well than if he were in a setted class and if possible he should do better. Clearly, ways must be found whereby those pupils who work quickly are not held back, those pupils who are unable to sit still and listen to a teacher for long have the opportunity of acquiring knowledge in more satisfactory ways and those pupils who need careful and detailed guidance can receive it.

Worksheets, now a household name, became the answer. It was clear that if instructions for practical work could be itemized in satisfactory language then an individual pupil ought to be able to get on at his own pace. Various types of worksheets have been written over the years and experience has revealed the poor quality and defects of our early efforts. Possibly the biggest difficulty in writing a Science worksheet is in expressing oneself succinctly, yet with adequate detail, in language which every pupil can understand. Very few teachers appreciate the limited vocabulary possessed by the average child of eleven, or even thirteen. Immediately it becomes apparent that if most of the lesson depends on the ability to read a worksheet, the non-reader or child with low reading age is in difficulty. Our answer to this was to use the school remedial department. Whereas many Science teachers feel that it is better to keep the child in the Science lessons, we believed that it was far better to allow him to receive concentrated tuition in reading and writing over a fairly short period and then return to the Science Department able to cope with the written material. Again our experiences have confirmed our faith in this course of action and in most cases one or two terms were

sufficient to enable backward pupils to acquire sufficient skill to return to normal lessons. It is true that he will have missed a fair amount of work but, as the emphasis is not on acquiring facts, this is not of devastating consequence. In the event many pupils were so keen to rejoin the classes that progress was really excellent and in one case a boy who was unable to read at eleven was later in a top Physics set in the fourth year. This particular example lends support to the argument that there are some potentially able scientists who can understand principles but who, when writing, have very poor powers of communication.

Ideally, it is desirable that different work-sheets be available for pupils of different abilities or from different social backgrounds, the basic differences between the sheets being in the form of language used. It can be argued with some justification that able pupils feel offended when confronted with language which even the weakest can comprehend. Although a selection of work-sheets is desirable, in practice we never got to the position where we had either the time or paper to do this. Provided that there is adequate work to do, the able pupil will be satisfied.

For the first year classes forty-four worksheets were devised and arranged in a number of series. Each series was based on related experiments and was designed to take, on average, about four weeks. The material included experiments in elementary Chemistry, Physics, and Biology, although no attempt was made to define them as such. In fact the emphasis was on an integrated treatment wherever possible. Nuffield Combined Science and the separate Nuffield subject texts provided source material, as did many traditional text-books.

A reference library was set up in each of the two laboratories, providing a variety of textbooks, background books and other relevant material. Wallcharts, both published and internally produced were also used to good effect.

The worksheets each attempted to extend fully the able pupils whilst still motivating the less able. To do this, experiments were designed for pupils to work at individually and all pupils carried out the same basic tasks.

Each experiment or series of short experiments was outlined on a pink sheet (the experiment sheet) and this was accompanied by a

second, white, sheet (the writing up sheet). The pupils were instructed to use their jotters (rough books) for noting the results of the experimental tasks and each pupil had a loose-leaf file in which the written work was recorded and retained. Examples of these types of sheets are included as appendices to this article.[1] The writing up usually consisted of a brief description of the experiment, some questions to answer, sentences to complete and sometimes a diagram to draw and/or label.

As a follow-up to each experiment or group of experiments, "further work" or "research" was included with clear instructions that this should only be done *"on the instructions of your teacher"*. The intention of this was to ensure that experiments were performed properly and as good a written account was produced as was appropriate to the child's ability. In fact we found that even the least able were anxious to do the further work. Although the allocation of further work was left entirely to the judgment of the individual teacher, it was found in practice to be difficult to stop the pupils doing it, however superficially in some cases. Nevertheless, the pupils were required to submit the written account of each experiment to the teacher for marking before being given permission or being instructed to do further work or proceed to the next experiment.

Clearly the teacher can get into concentrated discussion with one or two pupils and this must be avoided at all costs. Whilst there is no question that this can be of benefit to the individuals concerned, the main task of the teacher during such practical sessions is to "keep the show moving". He is required to take a quick glance at work presented for marking and ensure that it appears to be complete and of adequate standard; he has not the time to sit down and mark it on the spot. Experience showed that where teachers became involved in marking during the lesson discipline suffered as a result of pupils not knowing what to do next and standing around or interfering with others. The teacher is more a "Master of Ceremonies", ensuring that experiments are being carried out safely, chivying the slow and the time-wasters and allocating new experiments and homework, whilst at the same time encouraging the inquisitive to search for information and the answers to questions.

The same homework cannot, of course, be set to all pupils. Consequently before the end of the lesson the teacher must check with each pupil the stage he has reached and provide suitable further work. In the case of the able pupils this will probably be some "research" or "further questions" using books. For the less able it will probably be writing up the experiment that has just been completed. We did not consider that homework must necessarily be done at home and we encouraged pupils to use the school library for research. It should always be borne in mind that many pupils do not have books at home and that the use of local libraries is quite foreign to many youngsters. Tasks that are set should be set for a purpose and not merely as a means of filling the homework timetable. I believe that it is better to set useful tasks irregularly than to set irrelevant and meaningless ones every night. At the same time I believe that, with thought, the good teacher is able to provide useful extension work for most occasions. He must however be prepared to cross the subject boundaries.

I earlier indicated that two laboratories were allocated specifically for this first year work. When a series or "circus" of experiments was in use, each laboratory was set out with a number of working places for each experiment. If, for example, the series comprised eight experiments then five sets of each lot of apparatus would be available, making forty working places in all. It is clearly essential that the total number of places exceeds the number of pupils in the class in order to allow some flexibility for pupils to work at different speeds and to compensate for the different lengths of time that individual experiments take.

We set up the two laboratories at the start of a particular series with each working place having a "pink" instruction sheet "stuck" on the bench and covered by a self-adhesive transparent plastic. This ensured that water or chemicals did not damage the sheet and also that the pupils could readily see the number of the experiment to which the apparatus related. All apparatus was placed by the work-sheet and could readily be checked by a laboratory assistant before the end of a class. This was found to be of vital importance for the smooth running of the work. Not only did it ensure that all apparatus and consumable materials were available for the start of each lesson but also reduced to the minimum the number of items "mislaid" during lessons. Items such as magnets and compasses are favourites for youngsters' pockets and it is only by checking and being seen to check every item that stocks can be completely preserved.

By leaving the laboratories set up, the amount of work falling on laboratory assistants in setting up and removing apparatus is greatly reduced and this enables their efforts to be channelled into supervisory work. We found it helpful if not essential to have one assistant constantly working in one or other of the two first year laboratories. They could then not only provide further stocks of consumables and replace broken apparatus, but could also become involved in actually assisting pupils in their practical work. One young lady assistant enjoyed this work so much that she eventually left to take a three year teacher training course at the College of Education.

Whilst it is a matter of opinion as to whether pupils should normally sit down whilst doing practical work, our situations demanded that they remained standing. The limited size of the room meant that it was essential to separate the practical work from any writing up. Hence we provided about fifteen desks and chairs and situated these at one end of the room. Although this was equal to only half the number of pupils, we found that at any one time about half were occupied in practical work and the other half in writing up.

Inevitably some experiments are unsuitable for pupils to perform individually. In these cases demonstrations were performed either for the whole class or for a group of pupils who had reached a particular stage. The latter course of action is to be preferred since it enables the demonstration to be carried out at an appropriate time and makes it far more relevant.

Of the five periods per week allocated to each group it was recommended that four (two doubles) should normally be devoted to individualised practical work. The fifth period was to be used for discussion. This proved to be an extremely useful session when problems of general interest could be discussed, questions asked and the relevance of the experiments considered. Being only half an hour or so in length, it was not too long to maintain the interest of most of the pupils.

At the end of each series, a double period or more was spent discussing each experiment in turn and usually demonstrating them in order that pupils could check that their results were correct or the inaccuracies could be explained in terms of experimental errors or other factors. A summary sheet was then given to each pupil and he would be required to learn for homework the factual material. A standard test was then set to all pupils and this contained questions of varying levels of difficulty and format. Items included sentence completions, labelling diagrams, short answer questions and some multiple choice questions. The scripts were marked by the teacher and a mark (always out of twenty-five) recorded on special sheets which were kept in the staff-room. It is important that the Head of Department or his delegate keeps a close check on such records to ensure that all staff enter the marks of all tests in order that the progress of each and every pupil is monitored.

The other records maintained by the staff comprised grades for each experiment performed by the various pupils. Here two grades could be awarded, one for the basic work and a second for any "further work" done. In general it was not the policy to indicate to pupils the grades awarded, rather to write suitable and encouraging comments on their work. The records, however, ensured that at any time the teacher could check what a particular pupil had done and hence what should be attempted next. The record showing which pupils attempted further work and how well they did this provided evidence as to whether pupils were reducing their efforts during the course of the year. At the end of the year a final mark was arrived at and used as a basis for assessing potential for the various courses offered as options in later years. One important principle followed throughout our courses was that no lists of marks were read out in class. Although this is a point often overlooked by inexperienced teachers, a mark list can provide a crushing blow for a weak pupil who has worked really hard and done his best and yet obtained very few marks. It is far better to speak to the pupils individually and offer words of encouragement.

Unfortunately, when the pupils who followed the above scheme entered Year 2 it was no longer possible to allocate laboratories solely for their use. Consequently other ways had to be found to enable the same type of teaching to take place. The school timetable required three mixed ability tutor groups to come to Science at any one time. It was entirely a matter for the department as to the way in which the pupils were arranged. After considerable thought it was decided to attempt some team-teaching whilst at the same time maintaining much of the individualised learning which we had developed in Year 1. For this to be possible one double period

per week for each group was devoted to Biological Science, this being taught in a Biology laboratory, and the other two double periods to Physical Science. This meant that at a particular time we had two groups doing Physical Science and one group Biological Science. Rather than having apparatus permanently set up we had to rely on the laboratory assistants to put out the required materials etc., before each lesson or series of lessons involving Year 2 classes. As far as possible we encouraged the timetabler to block Year 2 classes so as to minimise the need for the getting out and putting away of apparatus.

Whilst it is desirable that a particular member of staff should be responsible for all of the Science of a particular class, the provision of team-teaching makes this not absolutely essential and gives flexibility to the teaching commitments of the individual members of the department. Our method, so far as Physical Science was concerned, was to have two adjacent laboratories available and use one for the experimental work (no stools available) and the other for writing up. The staff, by mutual agreement, would supervise the two rooms appropriately and assist pupils in the experiments and ensure that writing up was done quietly and sensibly. The success of this team-teaching depended to a large extent on the personalities of the two members of each team. Provided that each was willing to accept responsibility for all pupils and equally was not "possessive" over control of his "own" class, the system worked well. Where the odd teacher with weak discipline was involved it was often necessary for the other member to play a bigger part than was expected - but this was not a major problem. The team-teaching situation also means that, where appropriate, a class or group of pupils can be isolated for some particular purpose and a demonstration, for example, can be performed by a specialist. In general terms we attempted to include a biologist in each team of three and thus have a cross-section of specialist knowledge.

The 13+ Intake Year

After the reorganization of education in Hull our first pupils entered the school at the age of thirteen. It was apparent from our early approaches to a number of Middle schools that the scientific backgrounds of the pupils would vary greatly. We decided therefore to assume nothing and provide a concentrated introductory year for all pupils. Although this inevitably meant that some pupils would repeat work they had previously done, there seemed no other feasible and immediate solution, in view of the large number of feeder schools. It was therefore essential to provide worksheets which were designed for these older pupils and which, like our previous ones, enabled pupils to work individually in mixed ability groups.

A contact with the Science adviser for Fife introduced us to the Scottish Integrated Science Scheme and this material impressed us considerably. We examined the worksheets which have since been published[2] and decided that the layout was extremely good but that the instructions for the pupils were not suitable for mixed ability classes. Far too much reliance was placed on the ability of the pupil to design his own experiment and the instructions were insufficiently detailed for the average pupil. Nevertheless the sheets placed far less emphasis on written work and this enabled a greater number of experiments to be done in the one year available. Consequently we selected the topics which we liked, added our own favourites from previous work and wrote a complete set of about 150 worksheets[3].

This work was done well in advance of the required date by the three Heads of Department who consulted other members of staff for comments and suggested amendments. When all the sheets had been finalised, stencils were typed by either a laboratory assistant, who had been originally appointed with the knowledge that some typing might be involved in her work, or by one of the Heads of Department. A typewriter was purchased from the departmental capitation allowance; this proved to be of immense value and was constantly in use. It was agreed that each pupil should build up his own set of completed sheets and so envelope files were purchased by the department for this. The problem of storage of both blank worksheets and completed class sets was overcome by using computer-paper boxes acquired from a local source. The sheets currently in use were placed in the laboratories in wire shoe-racks which we acquired when they were being disposed of from the cloak-rooms.

It was decided that apparatus would need to be put out for particular classes and removed at the ends of sessions. To facilitate this we purchased small plastic seed trays and suitably labelled these for sets of apparatus. A three-tier trolley was made from a commercially available steel framework and this was used by the laboratory assistants to transport apparatus. Although, on occasions, we attempted to leave apparatus on side-benches in the laboratories, this usually led to problems of interference from pupils in other classes.

Although the intention of this introductory course was to enable pupils to work at their own paces, in practice some members of staff relied too much on class teaching. Whilst the pupils were certainly participating in the work through individual or group practicals, by keeping all pupils on the same experiment at one time it was felt that less was achieved than we would have liked. Certainly the scheme can work admirably and this was shown by the efforts of the majority of members of the staff.

After the Initial Year
In an eleven to eighteen school a combined Science course may be usefully pursued by all pupils for two or three years whilst in most thirteen to eighteen schools one year is the maximum that can be allocated to such a course. The reason for this is the demands often placed on pupils by external examinations. At the present time there is little doubt that there is a swing back in many schools to a General Science approach. It has long been realised that in most schools pupils have been unable to obtain a balanced Science course if they have wished to take a wide range of other subjects or study, for example, more than one foreign language. Equally, Science teachers have been increasingly influenced by the attractive teaching material provided in the Nuffield Secondary Science and Schools Council Integrated Science projects. Consequently more schools are now using a "General" Science syllabus for pupils of all abilities instead of for just the weaker brethren as was the case in the immediate past.

Our own work has fallen into two areas - a traditional General Science course and a Nuffield Secondary Science type of course. Both of these courses, however, have been geared to a mixed ability approach, although on a restricted basis. At no time at Sir Leo Schultz High School has the Science Department favoured complete mixed ability teaching beyond Year 3, although evidence obtained at some schools, e.g. Countesthorpe College, indicates that it can be done successfully. Our reasoning is that different abilities often select different courses suitable to their own abilities and interests. Hence our pupils effectively "setted" themselves to some extent. Nevertheless, once all the pupils following a General Science course were known, we deliberately ensured that a cross section of that ability range was included in each group.

Our early effort in the eleven to eighteen situation consisted of writing an individualised course based on the Mode 1 Yorkshire Regional CSE Board syllabus. The syllabus was broken down into the traditional sections of Heat, Light, Sound, Water, Electricity, Magnetism and Air and worksheets were written on each section. Each sheet contained some general information on the particular topic, experiment instructions, some questions and instructions for writing up. To go with each section was a sheet of further work and a summary sheet containing the important facts on that section. Several sets of worksheets for each section together with a similar number of sets of apparatus, were available and kept in cupboards which were suitably labelled with a list of all the apparatus and materials available. The lists ensured that a quick check could be carried out at the end of each lesson and before the pupils left the room. Much apparatus which could have disappeared was thus preserved. To prevent the worksheets getting torn, each was backed with stiff card and covered by an adhesive transparent material.

A pupil would select, or be allocated, a section of work and would then go through the experiments in order and do any related reading or writing. As in the case of the other courses already described, a reference library of suitable background and textbooks was set up in each laboratory. The teacher's role in this type of lesson is to assist the pupils where required and in particular to direct their experimental work and research so that each pupil is permanently engaged. Only when pupils are left with little work do discipline problems arise. Inevitably some experiments, e.g. the mercury barometer, are unsuitable for pupils to perform themselves and it was for this reason that we set up a demonstration room where a member of staff was situated with the sole job, for that lesson, of performing demonstrations. In this room a set of apparatus for each demonstration was assembled and pupils were encouraged to go in groups of three or four when they reached the appropriate point in their section of work.

Although the scheme was a great improvement on the formal teaching of General Science, we felt that there was much room for improvement in the subject content and decided therefore to prepare a Mode

3 syllabus and examination. This, I believe was probably our best piece of work.

Our intention was to provide a course in Science covering many aspects, the fundamental criterion for the inclusion of material in the course being "relevance". It was agreed that for the majority of pupils Science must be seen to be relevant to everyday experiences or world events. We utilized the Nuffield Secondary Science material to a large extent and also used a large number of other publications even to the extent of obtaining leaflets from breweries. Our course was designed for the last two years of compulsory education and was based on topics. Although integration between the various disciplines was desirable, no set route as recommended by the Nuffield Secondary Science was to be followed. Instead the course was to be taught by a team of teachers, each one of whom was to teach a number of the units, where possible in accordance with his or her own wishes. Units for Year 4 were each designed to take about eight weeks whilst those for Year 5 would take four weeks. Hence each pupil would study five topics in Year 4 and six in Year 5 (prior to public examinations). The first year of the course comprised five compulsory topics whilst pupils selected six topics from about eleven for the second year. Each member of the department wrote the worksheets for one or more units and in some cases provided individualised booklets containing background information, experimental details and questions. The approaches for the teaching of the different units varied but the attempt to cater for different abilities by individualising the work was a constant feature. The syllabus for this course is included as appendix 3.

Although it is early days to assess the success of the scheme, it would appear that the pupils enjoy the work and get far more out of it than they did from the previous scheme. Although it is probable that the least able are still doing little more than coming into contact with scientific ideas and they can spend lots of time copying from books, the scheme enables those with greater ability to tackle topics in great depth.

Flexibility as regards the breakdown of time spent on writing and practical work makes the course suitable for both boys and girls.

It is essential in this type of course to provide an appropriate examination at the end. Our wish was to allow those pupils who showed sufficient ability to obtain a Grade 5 or higher in CSE to enter for the examination. It was never intended that CSE should cater for all pupils below the GCE level and we believe that to enter all pupils is to abuse the examination. Nevertheless pupils are given until February in the final year to show their ability and only then is a decision taken on entries. The setting of the examination proved to be a difficult task and required all teachers to submit questions which were moderated by myself in order to obtain a reliable and valid examination.

Staffing

When discussing our work with colleagues from other schools I have frequently been told that they are unable to attempt mixed ability teaching because of staff resistance. I sympathise with their dilemma as it is clear that such an approach can only work if all the staff want it to work. We have always been in the fortunate position of being able to appoint new staff to do this sort of work. Only if enthusiasm was apparent at the interview did the Head appoint a particular applicant. At no time were we faced with an established departmental team who were unwilling to look at new ideas. Our close contacts with University Departments of Education and Colleges of Education have resulted in the recruitment of some excellent young teachers, a number of whom opted to join the staff after completing their teaching practice in the school.

There is no doubt that mixed ability teaching is an exciting and exacting task. The teacher has the satisfaction of obtaining excellent personal relationships with individual pupils and at the same time his discipline problems are reduced. This is not to say that the teacher can get away with little or no preparation for lessons. Although much of the work must be done before the start of a course rather than before a particular lesson, it is absolutely essential that the teacher knows precisely what each pupil is to do on each occasion. He must keep up-to-date records, he should mark all the work of each pupil regularly and above all he must have done sufficient background reading himself to have all the facts at his fingertips and know references to particular pieces of information which pupils are likely to require. In all it is a very demanding form of teaching but at the same time, when done well, most rewarding.

There is little doubt that few Colleges or University Departments have the experience through their staff to acquaint their students adequately with mixed ability techniques and even those students who have some knowledge of the theories find the work extremely energy consuming. Consequently a continuous process of in-service training is required in each school and it is here that the Head of Department can play a major part.

After teaching in a fairly traditional school where one was left in a classroom to do a job with a particular class and was virtually on one's own, I initially found it strange to work in a school with an "open doors" philosophy. By this I mean that it was quite normal and, indeed, an encouraged practice for the Heads of Department to go into other people's classes. This was not done with the intention of checking up on them, but rather to assist in the in-service training. The pupils were accustomed to regular visits and took for granted the assistance they might receive from "passers by". I encouraged other members of staff to come into my own lessons and I have no doubt that by this cross-fertilization of ideas we all benefited greatly. The other essential in a mixed ability teaching situation is to have regular departmental meetings where courses and methods are openly discussed. With all our courses, a weekly meeting at 4.00 pm was considered to be essential and in these it was customary for the author of a worksheet or the Head of Department to discuss the methods to be used in the classroom situation.

Possibly the key to successful mixed ability teaching is the willingness of staff to become "Scientists" rather than "Chemists", "Physicists" or "Biologists" and to educate themselves in the disciplines with which they are less familiar. The willingness to work as members of a team and the ability to accept constructive criticism in the right spirit are both facets of a successful department. The laboratory assistants are also key persons and are as much part of the team as the teachers. It is essential that they know precisely how to collect apparatus for new sections and how to maintain the apparatus which is constantly in use. It is essential that a typist is available to produce and duplicate the large number of worksheets which are an integral part of any such scheme; for one course alone we produced thirty-one kilometres of worksheet in one year!

Facilities and Equipment

It is clear that the types of course we pursued are demanding, not only in terms of staffing, but also in terms of paper, consumable materials and general apparatus. It is expensive to allow pupils to follow practically-based courses, to provide worksheets and all the necessary chemicals, living material and general apparatus. Unless money is made available to Science Departments it is difficult to see that useful gains can be made by changing from traditional methods. Our own efforts, however, do show that given the money, laboratory space, teaching time and adequate teaching and ancillary staff, considerable advantages can accrue from the type of approach outlined in this article.

Limitations of Mixed Ability Teaching

There is little doubt that the main criticism directed at mixed ability teaching is that it leads to mediocrity. Whilst I would certainly agree that this can be the case, I believe that we have shown that it is possible to achieve excellent results at all levels of ability using the technique. Our first genuinely comprehensive intake of 1968 completed their "O" level/CSE courses in 1973 and the examination results of these pupils were excellent, many achieving high grades at "O" level. Equally, the least able (non-examination) pupils performed far better than would have been expected in a traditional set-up. I believe the danger lies with the middle range of ability, but, provided that one is aware of this, then here too no lowering of standards will take place. The biggest difficulty is the provision of further work for the most able pupils and here much thought has to be given. It is very easy to allow these pupils to drift along producing excellent work and results on the basic material but not at the same time being fully extended. Constant attention must be given to the progress of the courses, and amendments should be made in the light of experience. No course will be perfect initially as curriculum development is an on-going process. Nevertheless, I believe that the considerable effort needed to establish mixed ability courses in Science is well worth making and the success of the resulting courses will be adequate reward in itself.

References

1 See Appendix 1

2 Scottish Integrated Science Worksheets - Heinemann

3 See Appendix 2

Experiment 3

Title: Making a solution

Apparatus

Check that you have the following:
A Bunsen burner, an asbestos board, a gauze, a tripod, a beaker, some
copper sulphate crystals, a glass rod.

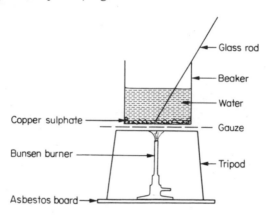

Instructions

1 Take the beaker to the tap and run into it about one inch of water.
2 Add a pinch of copper sulphate to the water and stir well using the
  glass rod.
3 In your jotter write down what happens to the copper sulphate.
4 Add another pinch and stir well.
  Continue doing this until *a little* copper sulphate remains on the
  bottom of the beaker.
5 Connect the Bunsen burner to the gas, and light it to give a medium
  flame.
6 Set up the apparatus as in the diagram.
7 Stir the water well, but do not allow it to boil.
8 After a few minutes remove the Bunsen burner.
9 In your jotter write down what has happened to the copper sulphate.

Write the following on a sheet of paper in your file.   White Sheet

Experiment 3
Title: Making a solution

Apparatus

A Bunsen burner, an asbestos board, a beaker, a glass rod, a gauge, a tripod, some copper sulphate crystals.

DRAW AND LABEL THIS DIAGRAM

Observations

Write a few sentences describing what you did in the experiment.
Now write down and complete the following sentences:
When the cold water was stirred, the copper sulphate .. ..
When the water was heated the remaining copper sulphate .. ..

Write down and learn the following
1. Water is a *solvent*
2. Copper sulphate is a *solute*
3. Copper sulphate *dissolves* in water and forms a *solution*
4. When no more copper sulphate dissolves, the solution is said to be *saturated.*

Additional work:

DO NOT DO ANY OF THE FOLLOWING UNTIL YOU HAVE SEEN YOUR TEACHER
1. At home choose a number of things, such as coal, dust, flour, sweets, bath salts, talcum powder and find out whether or not they dissolve in water.
2. Find out the names of some other solvents and what they are used for.

A Year 1 Worksheet for 13+ Entry

Name   .

SECTION 5   MIXING AND SEPARATIN

Sheet 2

Filtration and Evaporation

Instructions	Observations
1 Take as much of the mixture of sand and salt as will cover a penny. Put this in a beaker and add 50cm³ cold water. Stir the contents of the beaker. What do you see happening to the sand and salt?	
2 Fold a piece of filter paper and place this in the funnel. Set up the apparatus. Pour the contents of the beaker slowly into the funnel. (a) What is left on the filter paper? (b) What is left in the flask?	Filter funnel — Conical flask (a) (b)
3 Pour the contents of the flask into an evaporating basin. Heat this over the bunsen as shown, until *nearly* all the water has evaporated. Let the basin cool slowly. (a) What is left in the basin? (b) What has happened to the water?	Evaporating basin — Gauze (a) (b)
4 Explain carefully why it has been possible to separate the sand and the salt.	

In the filtration, the solid left on the filter paper is called the
RESIDUE. The liquid passing through is called the FILTRATE.

Appendix 3

Syllabus for Mode 3 CSE course in General Science

Year 4 Topics: (Compulsory)

Materials (Fuels and metals)
Life cycles
Communications
An environmental study
Man and microbes

Year 5 Topics: (Pupils select six)

Universe and space travel
Physics of movement
Cosmetic science
Simple genetics
Soil and food production
Automative science
Wines, spirits and beers
Electronics
Fabrics and Dyeing
An environmental study
Weather
Animal behaviour

Chapter 12
French

R.S. Walmsley

When I first came to Evelyns school as an assistant French teacher eight years ago it was designated a Secondary Modern school. There was a three form intake and a rigidly streamed system was operated for the first three years. All but the remedial children were expected to learn French for the first three years. In the fourth year, pupils opted for a so-called "academic" or a "non-academic" course. Needless to say French did not figure in the latter category, and all but a select few breathed a sigh of relief (echoed by the French teaching staff) and discontinued their learning of French in favour of other subjects.

The select few varied between 10 per cent and 20 per cent of any given year, a shamefully small percentage invariably taken from the "A" stream with a small number from the "B" stream. The proportion of CSE and "O" level passes was high and the whole educational exercise eventually seemed justified, provided that one was prepared to ignore the fact that eighty per cent of any given year group had started out with great enthusiasm, learning a new subject with all its flavour of foreign countries and different customs, only to discover that the subject was not, apparently, really included in the curriculum for their benefit.

Disillusionment was not slow to set in. In the first year every pupil was at least moderately enthusiastic. Indeed the "A" streams were a pleasure to teach, quick to respond to audio-visual techniques, capable of acquiring and retaining an extensive vocabulary, uninhibited when speaking aloud etc. This "ideal" state of affairs had usually deterioriated considerably by the end of the second year, with the onset of the growing-up period, and disintegrated by the third year - half the pupils having come to the conclusion that they were merely marking time until the obligatory learning of French was over. The other half of the "A" stream would of course become the examination group of the fourth year, but they learnt under great difficulties in the third year, the teacher of necessity being preoccupied with discipline in a group where interests became so sharply divided. There was a similar pattern of development with the "B" and "C" streams, but the cycle of deterioration was accentuated the lower down one went, a slower rate of learning, inability to memorise and retain new words and a lack of stimulation from more able pupils all contributing to this. One significant factor, however, was that even in the "C" streams there would always be a small but important minority who retained an interest in the subject despite all the odds against them. This group was indeed underprivileged, since this interest never had the chance of coming to fruition. This underlines the point that the desire to learn a foreign language does not depend upon academic ability at all - I suppose in the same way that a desire to go fishing or to collect stamps does not appeal to everyone and certainly does not depend on intelligence to be a rewarding experience. This argument would also seem to indicate that teaching mixed ability groups would not solve the wastage problem in language teaching - and this has now been demonstrated to be true in our school.

From the point of view of allocating staff to classes, teaching in streamed groups was bound to lead to difficult situations. Who was to teach the more able groups and therefore, from the teacher's point of view, the more rewarding groups? The problem usually resolves itself by a system where one took it in turns on a yearly basis to take the ablest groups. The week was spent in pleasant anticipation of the "high" spots in order better to endure the more frequent "low" spots. We accepted this situation with a fairly good grace, but in retrospect one wonders how a professional body could have justified it on educational grounds.

Teaching streamed groups produced the following clear results in our schools. Firstly, a streamed system did ultimately produce a small group of proficient language learners capable of achieving very good examination results at CSE and "O" level and ultimately "A" level. Secondly, this system overshadowed a significant percentage of average or below average pupils who might otherwise have benefited from learning a language.

I do not want to appear to be generalising about modern language teaching experiences - I am sure that many more able colleagues than myself do not neglect their less able pupils to the extent that we did at that time. However, frequent discussions with other language teachers have brought to light the existence of very similar problems in other schools but no two schools being alike it would be unwise to do anything other than discuss one's own situation in the hope that it has some general application.

After I had taught at this school for some years, two important changes took place; we acquired the word "Comprehensive" after the name of the school, and a new Headmaster introduced mixed ability grouping into the first year, these groups to be retained for the first three years of their school life. Owing to the retention by the local authority of our neighbouring Grammar school, there was no significant change in the academic ability of our new intake - an important stable factor when trying to judge the effects of so sweeping a change as the introduction of mixed ability grouping. Now, some five or six years later, I feel I can assess these effects, although as ever in teaching there are no single clear-cut conclusions.

I had understood from somewhere or someone that one of the advantages in teaching mixed ability groups was the mutual help given by the more able to the less able pupils. I had a strong premonition that this point would not be valid for language learning which is so completely teacher-centred in its initial stages - assuming one is using audio-visual, orally based teaching methods. My feeling on this point at least was justified by experience. This teacher-centredness perhaps explains why other subject teachers in our school, notably the Humanities subjects, adapted far more quickly and successfully to the mixed ability teaching situation, so much of their work being by its very nature pupil-centred. I also felt that the "mutual help" idea, if it were to succeed in modern language teaching, would depend for its success on a Utopian state of affairs where teaching groups were small. However, casting doubt on one claim does not invalidate the whole issue, and I am sure now that some truth does exist in this claim, although any help given by the more able is quite unintentional.

I would like to outline now in some detail various points that have emerged strongly since we introduced a mixed ability teaching system, since which time we have had a relatively stable teaching staff in the languages department - a prerequisite for the success of any scheme.

The painful task of choosing who should take the less able groups each year is obviated, since, for the first two years at least, the now twelve teaching groups in the first and second years are all more or less equal in ability. The corresponding improvement in morale amongst the teaching staff - especially probationers - is an enormous benefit in itself, and the results of this are quickly communicated to the pupils by way of more conscientious teaching and a more relaxed atmosphere. Staff become attached to certain groups, and there is often disappointment expressed that any setting will affect the composition of the existing groups.

Certain discipline problems in the first two years are largely eliminated since the potential trouble-makers are evenly spread throughout the year group. In any case I am now convinced that any system which relegates pupils for ever downwards is asking for the creation of discipline problems especially in a school where a form of selection at 11+ has already taken this step. I would not pretend of course that mixed ability grouping has in any sense solved all discipline problems, but one is at least dealing all the time with the tangible evil of problem individuals rather than the intangible resentment of a group which feels underprivileged.

There very soon emerged what ought to have been an expected phenomenon, in view of earlier comments, but which was for us an unlooked for justification of mixed ability teaching. It appeared during the course of producing a half-hour long playlet for a school performance. The play was appreciated by parents and thirteen year old sceptics alike, and great admiration was expressed for the high standard of fluency and pronunciation on the part of the cast, who were all first year pupils. It was only after the event that I discovered by chance conversation with colleagues that two out of the cast of seven had been attending remedial classes. The real importance of this comparatively trivial discovery was that it made us examine more closely the composition of our first and second year teaching groups, and the correlation between "intelligence" and the ability to learn a language. No dramatic revelations. The more able pupils in other subjects were nearly always the more able at French too. As usual there are a number of able pupils whose ability is not immediately apparent until they begin written work. But in each group there is always a significant percentage of pupils whom we at first take to be academically bright children (usually at oral work) but who later prove to be only of average or below average ability at other subjects. They possess a gift of oral fluency which the modern method of teaching French is suited to. It is quite proven in my mind that teaching a language in mixed ability groups creates an atmosphere in which a greater number of pupils of a wider ability range develop an interest in language learning than would have been the case in a streamed system. Neither does mixed ability grouping seriously affect the speed with which a group learns the language *in the initial stages of secondary education*, that is to say, the first year and the first half of the second year.

As I said earlier, this beneficial effect upon the less able is not achieved by any conscious help from the more able pupils, but merely from the creation of a situation in which this learning may take place. Perhaps the reason for this lies less with the pupils of a particular group - who are in the position to compare their respective abilities in *all* their subjects - than with the language teacher who cannot compare the abilities of his pupils in other disciplines and is not, therefore, in a position to prejudge their likely abilities in language learning. The teacher therefore rewards and encourages a group's best performers without even being aware of a given pupil's academic ability in other subjects.

It is sometimes said that language learning is not the prerogative of the intelligent, so that by creating mixed ability groups we are taking the first step in playing down the intelligence factor which after all is too much of an unknown quantity in learning habits.

I have outlined certain advantages that we feel have emerged clearly over the past few years. Our experiences so far have been quite convincing enough to preclude the possibility of ever returning to a streamed system in any shape or form. Why, with all its apparent advantages, does the mixed ability system of grouping for language learning seem to break down in the latter part of the second year of secondary education?

I think the fault is only accidentally to do with mixed ability grouping itself. By the end of the second year and certainly the third year, ubiquitous puberty has set in. The spontaneous oral approach to language teaching is no longer feasible; pupils become self-conscious, resentful of childish repetition (as they see it) and critical of work. The teacher's reaction is predictable. There has to be a return to a more formal approach, more written work, more abstractions to explain the language structure - all the factors indeed which emphasise the difference in pupils' mental abilities.

It is at this stage that the harm begins. Brighter pupils do become bored with the slower pace. Of this I am sure. This is the greatest disservice we could ever render to our intelligent youngsters. It is not because classes are mixed in ability that this comes about, but rather because of the changing demands of teaching methods when dealing with adolescents rather than children. But I no longer believe that it is wise to enforce mixed ability grouping beyond a point when the majority - or even an important minority - are no longer benefiting, out of sadly misplaced egalitarian principles. "Comprehensive" education was surely never designed to make every one equally proficient in the same subjects.

When first introduced in our school the pastoral groups created by random grouping determined the composition of the teaching groups up to the end of the third year - in common with many other schools I believe. Thereafter pupils opted for the subjects of their choice. What soon became obvious was that the re-grouping had not solved the wastage problem - only a slightly larger percentage of pupils opting for continuing foreign language studies into the fourth and fifth years. In this area the problem is not confined to Secondary Modern or Comprehensive schools. Grammar schools suffer from the same problem where an option system of subjects operates, reinforcing the view which I have held for some time that pure language learning as an end in itself does not have a universal appeal, but has a very strong appeal to a minority group. By the third year, pupils either like or dislike the subject. There is very little neutral feeling on the matter. With a willing class, regardless of ability, a great deal of learning can take place.

The second thing to emerge at this point was how successful the mixed ability grouping system had been in recruiting from the ranks of the pupils of average ability or below. Admittedly some of them set out in the fourth year with no illusions that their examination results would be outstanding, but the willingness to learn was there. This group of children has to be catered for by a suitable examination.

Examination requirements meant that fourth year classes were setted where the number of pupils involved warranted this. In the case of a second language option - Italian in this instance - where there were insufficient pupils to warrant the formation of two set groups, the teaching group was very mixed in ability. The less able ones benefited. Nevertheless the overall result was a disaster, the main offender being not the grouping but the exigencies of examination techniques. But the brighter pupils know that it is they who suffer. The disadvantages of teaching at a slower pace are felt therefore in the fourth and fifth year.

In recent years our language examination results at fifth year level have been poorer. I am not a great advocate of the examination system but it is a factor which cannot be ignored when determining our teaching groups. At the present time a good examination result is still the just reward of a pupil's hard work and the key to his future. The greatest disadvantages of teaching mixed ability groups higher up in the school, now aggravated by the raising of the school leaving age, are felt by the more intelligent pupils. The one risk aspect of the whole matter is this creation of a new group of underprivileged - the intelligent pupils, capable of academic success.

I am sure many a teacher foresaw these risks, but possible solutions are slow to come, bound up as they are with problems of time-tabling and the need to develop curricula within language departments.

A Swing Back to Setting Groups

Over the past two years, mixed ability grouping as a system rigidly imposed on the first three years has gradually been eroded in our school. The impossibility of teaching pure language work to mixed ability groups of third year pupils - who are a perennial problem at the best of times - soon brought about the relaxation of principles in favour of practicalities. The third year was arranged into two bands of eight teaching sets, there being a top French set in each band. We have tried various unsuccessful formulas on the lower sets - introduing a second language for one year, or relying on individual staff to muddle through teaching what they could about France or Europe in general. The main fault here was lack of concerted effort and real aims, and the deliberate policy of not teaching any language to the "unwilling". At least this system allowed us to ensure that all those pupils who wanted to learn French could do so in relative peace, but it left us with the feeling that we were somehow failing in our duty.

This year the erosion of random mixed ability grouping has reached down to the second year in a way which smatters suspiciously of a return to a selective system. The year group is divided into two bands, as is the third year. In conjunction with the Science and Maths Departments, the Modern Languages Department will teach "creamed off" top sets in each band, the other sets remaining mixed in ability. The top set was selected on the basis of general ability and IQ in an attempt to satisfy the needs of all three departments at a single stroke without complicating the time-tabling. I mention this trend merely to show how under certain pressures the gospel of mixed ability teaching can quickly revert to a compromise position - not one that our department approved of either. We had in fact asked for a "band" system as in the third year which would enable us to set at our will at a later stage in the second year. Instead we find ourselves with a system which is rigid, because its formation is bound up with the organisation of two other departments.

There are two grave faults. Firstly the sorting out has taken place at far too early a stage, before the mixed ability groups have settled down into teaching units and at least two terms before the beneficial aspects of teaching mixed groups cease to predominate. Secondly, and most vital, many of our promising pupils of average ability would suddenly find themselves bereft of the encouragement of their more able friends. Negotiations had to be opened immediately to salvage as many of these pupils as possible, but I have a strong suspicion that we shall have increased teaching problems in the second year. I hope there is an object lesson here for someone!

Although it might appear that in our case events have completed almost a full circle, this is in fact very far from the truth. The real revolution brought about by introducing mixed ability grouping has left an indelible mark upon our way of thinking. A return to streaming is unthinkable. Neither do we try to select teaching sets on the basis of the pupils' overall academic ability - at least in the first three years. Even our "top" sets contain a fair proportion of average ability pupils, selected for their enthusiasm for the subject rather than their accuracy. In the same way the non-language groups in the third year have a proportion of bright pupils who have no natural inclination to study French.

To conclude this part of the discussion I would sum up by stating that a mixed ability system of teaching a foreign language is ideal for the first year, still beneficial for most of the second year but untenable in the third year; that, where the subject is being taken to examination level in the fourth and fifth years, teaching requirements demand a system of setting according to the academic abilities of the pupils.

Possible Solutions - the Introduction of a European Studies Course
The educational problems involved in teaching a modern language to pupils of all abilities can have no single solution. Mixed ability grouping goes a long way to alleviating the difficulties in the first two years of secondary schooling. But I believe now that a language department must expand its outlook if it is to survive in a meaningful way. I think that the main barrier for too long has been the accepted notion that, since all pupils should have the opportunity of learning a language, all pupils should receive identical instruction; that what a schoolchild should understand by "foreigners" by the time he has left school should be arrived at in an identical manner.

Cultural exchanges as frequently as possible and on as many levels as possible with our neighbouring countries are the ideal way to break down prejudices and to develop understanding. Foreigners have to be seen to be normal human beings, to be lived with if possible. Since this kind of exchange is still impractical and expensive for the average youngster, then at least our school courses should have such aims in mind. Learning a language, even for the linguistically able, is a barren experience if it never leaves the school classroom, and an exchange visit of some sort is vital if the course is to be successful. If, for many

pupils, a European Studies course (call it what you will) can further
the aims of understanding of other nations in a way that a language
course does not, then surely it is more desirable to teach such a
course? Many of our secondary pupils at the end of their second
year have been going through the motions of learning French for
four, or maybe five, years, and it is by then apparent to them, if not
always to those teaching them, that they will never become fluent
by learning a language in a classroom. So why continue the struggle?

We decided that the solution might be to introduce a well-organised
European Studies course at the third year stage for pupils who
wanted to opt out of learning French. It is hoped to make it into an
option subject in the fourth and fifth years leading to a Mode 3
CSE examination. The course will open with a discussion on
"Prejudices". It is to contain some elementary "useful" language
work, not restricted to French alone. Except for about 20 per cent of
our more able linguists, the whole of the second year was given the
option to choose between carrying on with French or taking
European Studies. To our infinite surprise, and secret relief perhaps,
much less than half (about 35 per cent) of the year group opted for
European Studies. It is too early to judge the worth of such a course
educationally speaking, but it will certainly relieve many of the
tensions which build up during the third year.

From the point of view of the main issue of this chapter, it is
important to point out that the European Studies groups will not
consist of the "throw-outs" from the French group, as has happened
all too often in the past. There are in them a greater proportion of
intelligent, academically able boys - rather than girls. But considering
that there are more pupils of average or below average ability than
above in a school such as ours, then we have certainly preserved the
main principles of integration of ability, whilst catering for different
tastes as well.

Preserving random mixed ability grouping in the first two years of
secondary schooling has left us in the third year with a large residue
of pupils of all abilities who are still willing to tackle pure language
work. They will, however, be setted. In each of our two "bands",
there is a "top" set with large numbers of pupils in it, while the
second French set is much smaller (about twenty pupils) as are the
two European Studies groups. I believe that such flexibility within

a department is very necessary if the maximum benefit is to be derived from mixed ability teaching, since it is obvious that it is where groups are smallest that most help can be given. Such a system allows one to judge in individual cases which set a child would best be suited to. Often it is better to place a child of average ability in a lower set, whereas another child of perhaps less ability would benefit more from being in a top set.

Teaching Material

No publisher as far as I can discover has yet managed to produce a French course that is ideally suited to mixed ability groups, although a number claim to have done so. Indeed most of the courses available seem to be aimed at round about genius level. I am sure that a teacher, or group of teachers, could corner the market in this field, if they so wished.

We have found that it is constantly necessary to produce our own material to cope with the demands of mixed ability teaching. The basic courses need expanding with preliminary exercises and exercises to reinforce what has been learnt. Sketches are needed to clarify difficult vocabulary visually and so on. An overhead projector is a great help. And a language laboratory, of course, is the ideal instrument for teaching pupils who have different learning speeds. Group work within a classroom often manages to produce the miracle of learning that a teacher hardly ever manages to achieve; an able pupil with a set task or with a question and answer sheet is put in charge of a group of three or four pupils. Less able pupils will frequently respond much more easily in this situation than they will to a teacher in front of a whole class. Here again the principle French courses on the market rarely include this kind of work and the teacher has to develop his own material. Group work seems to be the natural instrument to use in a mixed ability class, so long as it is not relied upon too heavily.

One of our department said that he thought the most important change brought about by teaching in mixed ability groups was that he felt his imagination and resourcefulness had been stretched to their limit for the first time in his career. This fact illustrates that, once undertaken, while mixed ability teaching may benefit many less able pupils, it certainly gives the language teacher far greater insight into the problems of learning a language and the methods by which a language should be presented to children. The mental effort made by the teacher in presenting a foreign language clearly and in an uncomplicated manner must be to the advantage of all pupils regardless of their ability.

Once the step of introducing mixed ability grouping has been taken and the way of life has been established - at least in the junior section of a Secondary school - one does not pose the question whether such a system is successful or not, one talks about the problems of how best to use the advantages gained thereby to achieve the aims of language teaching.

As I have indicated, I believe the answer lies in some form of curriculum development. In adopting European Studies we are not being originators, of course, but at least such a course can be adapted to the particular needs of our pupils. This helps to solve the main dilemma in language teaching today, which turns out to be not how intelligent should a child be to learn a language at school but how can the real aims of teaching a language best be served in the case of each individual pupil.

Index